P9-BYZ-897

Hammond's County Map of Michigan
(Southern Peninsula)
Copyright by C.S. Hammond & Co., N.Y.

SCALE OF MILES

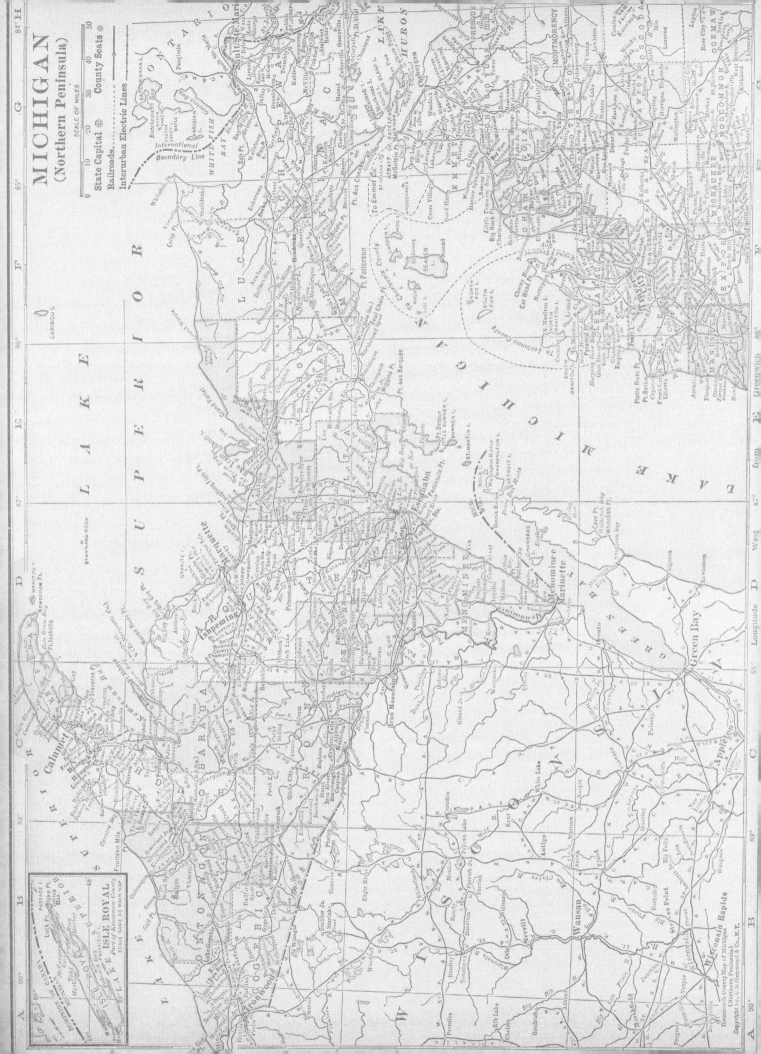

MICHIGAN
(Northern Peninsula)

SCALE OF MILES

State Capital ⊛
County Seats ⊙
Railroads
Interurban Electric Lines

International Boundary Line

LAKE SUPERIOR

LAKE HURON

LAKE MICHIGAN

GREEN BAY

WISCONSIN

ONTARIO

LAKE ISLE ROYAL
Part of Keweenaw County
SCALE SAME AS MAIN MAP

Copyright by C. S. Hammond & Co., N.Y.

Fork in the Road

with Eric Villegas

HURON RIVER PRESS

Fork in the Road

with

Eric Villegas

Copyright © 2007

All rights reserved. No part of this book may be reproduced in
any manner without the express written consent of the publisher,
except in the case of brief excerpts in critical reviews and articles.

All inquiries should be addressed to:
Huron River Press
308½ South State Street, Suite 30
Ann Arbor, Michigan 48104
www.huronriverpress.com

Food photography: Mark Thomas, Grand Rapids, Michigan
Photography assistant: Bob Hazen
Food and prop stylist: Loretta Gorman
Book design: Savitski Design, Ann Arbor, Michigan
Michigan location photography: Mike Savitski, Steve Klein, Ken Scott, Dana Owen
Postcards courtesy of Peter Sparling
Front cover image of Eric Villegas courtesy of Sarah Frank/*The State News*

Printed and bound in China

10 9 8 7 6 5 4 3 2 1

Library of Congress Cataloging-in-Publication Data

Villegas, Eric, 1959-
  Fork in the road with Eric Villegas.
    p. cm.
  ISBN 1-932399-17-8
  1. Cookery, American. 2. Cookery--Michigan. I. Fork in the road with
Eric Villegas (Television program) II. Title.
  TX715.V626 2007
  641.5973--dc22
                              2007027767

In loving memory of my mother Martha Hortensia Villegas Rollano

and to my father Alfonso Anastacio Villegas Loaiza...

whose unconditional love and generosity is almost embarrassing...

Even though my name is on this book as the author (me, an author — who woulda thunk it?!?!), writing a cookbook is truly a team effort and when that cookbook is the companion book to a TV show well, the effort is nothing less than Herculean.

I would like to start by thanking my good friend and business partner in "Fork". Scott Allman is the man behind the lens so to speak and brings "Fork" to life. To Andy our executive producer, the cast and crew of "Fork," Steve and Dick on cameras, Connie in makeup, the original kitchen angel Lil' KeeeUm and the angels that followed Biggie, Ben and Maija.

To Lori "lulu" Mahoney, my dining room manager and my friend who "drives the bus" while I am scampering off here and there always working on some project, and the individual that accomplished the expert Michigan beverage pairing that accompany the recipes . . . the entire staff of Restaurant Villegas past and present for their help and patience during the shoots as well as the restaurant guests who endured the same — but had to pay for it!

To DanaO for your unending support and taking on multiple jobs with grace and patience, from personal assistant and photographer to prep cook and designated driver . . . to Sam Spiegel for your unique insight into the world of books and publishing . . . to Steve and Shira Klein of Huron River Press who guided me through the trials and tribulations of such a huge project, who started as publishers and became friends . . . to Mike, Loretta, Mark and Bob for their talent in bringing the design, food and photos to life . . . to Peter Cronk and Charles Marquis for their guidance with all the legalese . . . to Trisha, Kay and Don whose generosity and support in the early days will never be forgotten . . . to all of "Forks" generous product sponsors and underwriters past and present . . . to all of the magical mitts and yoopers, farmers, ranchers and culinary artisans that make "Fork" a pleasure to shoot and are the true inspiration behind the recipes . . . last but certainly not least to all of the forkies, the kulinary katz-n-kittenz, the great lakes gastronauts that still keep watching the show regardless of how ridiculous I appear.

unkle e and Scott Allman

Contents

Middle of the Mitt

Bolivian Macaroni and Cheese 82

Quesadilla of Huitlacoche with
White Cheddar Cheese 84

Grilled Lamb with Mint Horseradish Glaze on
Warm White Bean Salad 85

Hickory Smoked Tomato Salsa 87

Roasted Garlic Purée 88

Chicken Sugar Beet Skewers with Maple Smoked
Jalapeño and Lime Glaze 91

Great Lakes White Shrimp Ceviche with Smoked
Tomatoes and Honeycrisp Apples 92

Grilled Ears of Michigan Sweet Corn with
Black Truffles 95

Michigan Beer Bread 96

Michigan Double Sweet Corn Chowder 98

White Shrimp with Garlic 99

Popcorn Shrimp 101

Popcorn Flour 101

Sweet Potato Taco with
Hickory Smoked Tomato Cream 102

Wood Roasted Pumpkin Risotto 104

Great Lakes White Shrimp Stuffing 105

Shrimp Stuffed Mushrooms 105

Carrot Couscous with White Shrimp and Chives 107

Fried Chicken and Buttermilk Waffles with
Thyme Lime Honey 108

Buttermilk Cornmeal Waffles 110

Minted White Chocolate Truffles 111

Turkey Cranberry Sausages 112

Mashed Sweet Potatoes with Horseradish 112

Poached Breast of Chicken with Fresh Carrot and
Ginger Sauce 113

Fresh Carrot Sauce with Ginger 113

Potato and Cheese Ravioli Topped with
Mixed Vegetable Vinaigrette 115

Mixed Vegetable Vinaigrette 116

Big Soft Pretzels 117

Spicy Chicken Wings with
Clancy's Fancy Hot Splash 119

Idaho Potato "Pommes Frites" 120

Cream of Grilled Tomato Soup 121

The Thumb

Cheese Fondue with Hard Apple Cider 125

Barbecue Beef Brisket 126

Basic Barbecue Rub 127

Chilled Spelt, Sweet Corn and Tomato Salad 128

Lake Effect Jumbo Sea Scallops with Hard Apple Cider
Butter Sauce 131

Hard Apple Cider Butter Sauce 132

Fromage Blanc 132

Wood Roasted Great Northern White Bean "Hummus"
with Two Garlics and Tahini 133

Michigan Inspired "Choucroute Garni" 134

Shirt Steak Fajitas with Michigan Ale and
Apple Cider Marinade 137

Gluten-Free Cream Biscuits 138

Maple Sage Breakfast Sausage 140

Maple Sage Sausage "Gluten-Free" Gravy 141

Grilled New York Strip Steaks with Coffee Chili Rub 143

Michigan Steamed Brown Bread with Dried Cherries
and Walnuts 144

Baked Michigan Navy Beans with Smoked Bacon,
Chiles and Cocoa 146

Maple Corndogs 147

Grilled Romaine Salad with Smoked Tomatoes,
Maytag Blue and Maple Spiced Nuts 149

Maple Rosemary Roasted Spiced Nuts 149

The U.P.

Great Lakes Pantry

Fork in the Road with Eric Villegas is not a "normal" cooking show and consequently this companion book is not your "normal" cookbook. For example, you normally would find recipes categorized by course or perhaps ingredients. It's not unusual to find recipes listed by season, but Michigan, my kulinary katz-n-kittenz is unique, which makes the show unique and of course makes this book well — unique. 🥔 We took the liberty of categorizing our state for our culinary purposes both agriculturally and geographically, with chapters covering Freshwater, The Fruit Belt, Middle of the Mitt, The Thumb, The U.P., and The Great Lakes Pantry — all unique, all pure Michigan. 🥔 "Fork" has been in production for five years at the time of this writing and even though I had always dreamed of writing a cookbook, I never thought I would ever get the chance to do so. So, for five years traveling around the state of Michigan meeting the farmers, ranchers and culinary artisans that make the mitt an incredible place to work, live and eat I came up with recipes inspired by the people I met, and the products I tasted, but not once did I ever think about how I would organize them.

All I was interested in was how to best showcase a particular product to show off its regional attributes — sometimes in a classic recipe from America or abroad, sometimes creating something new by merging the best of both worlds with classic culinary technique from around the world with our incredible local products. These new dishes aren't meant to replace the originals, but instead, show the reader what is possible and encourage each cook to come up with their own recipes, based on the foods around them, wherever they may live. ☐ This is by no means meant to be the definitive work on the foods of Michigan. Even after 5 years, it really only scratches the surface of what you might find in your own travels. Some of your favorites are probably missing and that doesn't mean that we weren't aware of them; we just haven't had the time to get there — the mitt is a big place! Rest assured however, as I'm writing this we are currently in production of a brand new season of "Fork", with great new shows that might include muskrat, thimbleberries, ice fishing and wild rice. The list keeps on growing which is a tribute to the magical mitten, which of course means, I need to write another book!

Sometimes referred to as inland seas, the Great Lakes are the largest grouping of freshwater on planet earth. The five bodies that make up the great lakes are Superior, the largest by volume and the deepest, which in 1975 took the lake freighter Edmund Fitzgerald and all 29 hands 20 miles off Whitefish Point in the most famous marine disaster (and popular tune) in the history of Great Lakes Shipping. Lake Michigan is the second largest in volume and third largest by area. It also has the distinction of being the only Great Lake located entirely in the USA. Lake Huron is the third largest by volume and second largest in area and is home to Manitoulin Island, the largest freshwater island in the world. Lake Erie is the smallest by volume and also the most shallow. Because of its lack of depth it is also the warmest and most biologically productive of all the lakes. Finally, Lake Ontario, the second smallest

Freshwater

volume-wise and smallest in area and probably because of this the lake has frozen over twice, once in the winter of 1874–75 and once in February of 1934. It is also the only Great Lake that does not border Michigan.   An anglers paradise, the lakes offer a four billion dollar a year industry with the big catches of salmon, whitefish, smelt, lake trout and walleye finding their way onto dinner tables in the mitt and across the country through commercial and native American fishing. In addition to the obvious fishing opportunities, there is also the bottled water industry that benefits from our freshwater and the not so obvious "lake effect." This peculiar weather phenomenon in conjunction with snow almost always conjures up the "Great Grey Funk." This synonym for winter is caused by cold air passing over warmer water leaving the southeastern shores of the lakes almost constantly overcast during certain conditions.

Boardman River, Michigan

Freshwater Whitefish Chowder with Bacon, Potatoes and Basil

In a large, heavy bottomed saucepan or Dutch oven over medium heat cook the bacon for 10 minutes or until the bacon is crisp and has rendered its fat. Remove the crisp bacon and reserve.

In same pan add the onions to the rendered bacon fat with the butter and bay leaves. Turn up the heat to medium-high and sweat the onions for 7 to 8 minutes, until they are soft and translucent. Add the herbs, potatoes, and Roasted Garlic Purée. Cover with the Fish Stock and season with the salt and pepper.

Simmer the chowder base for about 15 to 20 minutes or until the potatoes are just cooked and the broth is rich and flavorful.

Add the crème fraîche to the base and stir to blend. Submerge the fillets of whitefish into the base making sure the broth covers the fish and gently simmer the chowder another 5 minutes or until the fish is just cooked through. Taste the chowder for seasoning and adjust if necessary.

Gently transfer the broth to a large serving bowl and carefully top with the fillets.

Drizzle in the lemon juice to taste, top with the Basil Compound Butter and garnish with the Chowder Crackers.

Serve immediately.

Recommended beverage: Shady Lane Chardonnay

Serves 4

¼ pound thick cut Maple Cured Hickory Smoked Bacon, coarsely chopped, or similar, page 153

1 whole onion, peeled and halved lengthwise, cut julienne

3 tablespoons unsalted sweet butter

4 whole bay leaves

8 leaves fresh basil, chopped

3 pounds Yukon Gold potatoes, washed and cut into ½-inch chunks

2 tablespoons Roasted Garlic Purée, page 88

1 quart Fish Stock, page 172

1½ cups crème fraîche or heavy cream

4 fresh whitefish fillets, skinned, boned, and trimmed

1 whole lemon, juiced

sea salt

black pepper, freshly ground, to taste

Compound Butter, page 178, add basil per recipe instructions

Chowder Crackers, page 175

unkle e's ramblings on cha-dahh!

Arguably no one American dish has been subjected to more abuse than the classic New England chowders. And the recipe I offer you now is by no means authentic, but has the virtue of being true to the spirit and style of the original clam, cod and lobster chowders from America's east coast. Chowder or "cha-dahh" is a hearty one pot dish and when properly prepared is more of a stew than a soup and definitely not meant for a measly 4-ounce cup! Take the time to make this freshwater whitefish chowder flavored with Maple Cured Hickory Smoked Bacon and don't forget to bake up a batch of the Chowder Crackers!

Planked Fresh Water Whitefish Stuffed with Wild Rice and Shiitake Mushrooms

Serves 4–6

1 whole, large Great Lakes whitefish, or similar, head and tail on with the interior bones removed

sea salt, to taste

black pepper, freshly ground, to taste

1 large untreated cedar plank or shingle

¼ cup extra virgin cold pressed olive oil

¼ cup Lemon Vinaigrette, page 187

FOR THE STUFFING

¼ cup extra virgin cold pressed olive oil

1 medium red onion, peeled and cut julienne

1 cup shiitake mushrooms, preferably from Michigan, stemmed and sliced

¼ cup Roasted Garlic Purée, page 88

¼ cup flat leaf parsley, chopped

1 tablespoon fresh thyme, chopped

1 cup green onions, chopped

sea salt, to taste

black pepper, freshly ground, to taste

1 cup long grain white rice, cooked

1 cup Great Lakes wild rice, cooked and drained

½ cup Lemon Vinaigrette, page 187

Clancy's Fancy Hot Sauce, or similar, to taste

Season the whitefish inside and out with salt and pepper. Grill the cedar plank on one side to get nice black marks, (Without a grill, heat the plank for 10 minutes in the preheated 400 degree F oven to "cure" the plank.) and then rub down the cooking side (grilled side) of the plank with a little olive oil.

FOR THE STUFFING

In a large, heavy bottomed sauté pan, over medium-high heat add the olive oil and the sliced red onions. Cook the onions until translucent. Add the mushrooms and sauté for 2 to 5 minutes, follow with the Roasted Garlic Purée, parsley, thyme, and green onions. Season to taste with the salt and pepper.

Reduce heat to medium and add the cooked white and wild rices to the mushroom mixture, blend with the Lemon Vinaigrette and hot sauce to taste. When the mixture is warmed through and thoroughly seasoned, remove from heat and reserve.

TO ASSEMBLE

Placed the whole fish on the grilled and oiled side of the plank. Stuff the cavity of the whitefish with the cooled wild rice stuffing. Drizzle the top of the fish with some of the Lemon Vinaigrette. Place the plank on a suitable cookie sheet or roasting pan and place in the oven.

Baked the stuffed whitefish for 25 to 50 minutes (depending on the size of the fish) or until the skin is charred, the flesh is cooked, and the stuffing is hot.

For a spectacular presentation serve the whole stuffed whitefish on the hot plank with Lemon Vinaigrette on the side.

Recommended beverage: Chateau Chantel Chardonnay

Great Lakes Muffuletta

Serves 6–8

1 large red onion, peeled

1 cup cooked artichoke hearts packed in oil, drained well

½ cup roasted bell peppers

½ cup capers

⅓ cup red wine vinegar

sea salt, to taste

black pepper, freshly ground, to taste

1 teaspoon vinegar

4 whole eggs

1 large artisan focaccia loaf

½ cup Basil Walnut Pesto, page 185

2 cups romaine lettuce, shredded

4 fresh cow's milk mozzarella balls, sliced

4 heirloom tomatoes, preferably from Michigan, sliced

12 ounces smoked whitefish, preferably from Michigan, boned and flaked

8 white anchovy fillets, drained, or similar

Slice the peeled red onion as thinly as possible. Slice the artichoke hearts similarly to the onions. In a small bowl combine the sliced onions, artichokes, bell peppers, capers and red wine vinegar. Season to taste with sea salt and black pepper. Mix well and reserve for at least 15 minutes for the flavors to meld and the onions to wilt.

Hard-boil the eggs, starting with cold water and a teaspoon of vinegar in a small saucepan. Bring to a boil and cook for 3 minutes. Remove from heat and let the eggs remain in the hot water for 10 minutes. Peel, slice and reserve.

TO ASSEMBLE

Slice the foccacia in half horizontally. Spread the pesto evenly between top and bottom. Starting with the bottom half of the foccacia, cover it with the shredded romaine lettuce followed by the fresh mozzarella cheese, artichoke/onion mixture, and tomato slices. Season the tomatoes with some salt and pepper. Follow with smoked whitefish, sliced hardboiled eggs and finish with the anchovy fillets.

Cover the muffuletta with the reserved top of the foccacia. Wrap the sandwich very tightly in plastic wrap then wrap tightly in foil.

Store overnight in the refrigerator topped with a heavy skillet, heavy plate or even a brick to compress.

Remove from refrigerator, slice and serve.

I find that an egg slicer works equally well on fresh balls of mozzarella. Both hard boiled eggs and fresh mozzarella have similar textures and the thin wires found in egg slicers do a great job of consistent slicing as well as keeping the eggs and cheese stable during cutting.

Smoked Whitefish Cakes with Sweet Peppers, Smoked Jalapeños and Cilantro

In a heavy bottomed non-stick skillet heat 1 tablespoon oil over moderately high heat until hot but not smoking and sauté bell peppers and onions until softened. Cool and reserve.

In a bowl stir together the cooled bell peppers and onion mixture, cilantro, mayonnaise, Lake Effect Seasoning, jalapeños, Roasted Garlic Purée, 2 tablespoons of the Chowder Cracker crumbs and salt until well combined.

Gently fold in the whitefish trying to keep the pieces as big as possible and chill 20 minutes.

With a 2-ounce ice-cream scoop or ¼-cup measure, scoop fish mixture into 8 portions and pat each into ¾-inch thick disk. Spread remaining cracker crumbs on a sheet of wax paper and gently press each whitefish cake into them, turning it, to coat evenly. To help prevent crumbling during cooking chill whitefish cakes, covered loosely, at least 1 hour and up to 1 day.

Preheat oven to 375 degrees F.

In a heavy bottomed non-stick 12-inch skillet heat 1 tablespoon oil over moderately high heat until hot but not smoking and sauté half of whitefish cakes until golden brown, 3 to 5 minutes. Turn the cakes carefully and brown other sides. Transfer sautéed whitefish cakes carefully to a baking sheet. Add remaining tablespoon oil to skillet and sauté remaining whitefish cakes in same manner. On baking sheet bake all whitefish cakes 6 minutes, or until heated through.

Serve white fish cakes hot from the oven with Whole Egg Jalapeño Mayonnaise.

Recommended beverage: Good Harbor M. Foch Rose

—€ These whitefish cakes are made with lots of smoked whitefish and not much filler, consequently they require gentle handling during cooking.

—€ Trying to keep the whitefish pieces as big as possible helps give the cakes nice big chunks of fish.

Serves 4

3 tablespoons extra virgin cold pressed olive oil

1 whole red bell pepper, diced

1 whole yellow bell pepper, diced

1 medium red onion, peeled and diced

¼ cup fresh cilantro, chopped

¼ cup Whole Egg Mayonnaise, page 183, or commercial product of your choice

2 tablespoons Lake Effect Seasoning, page 188

2 whole Hickory Smoked Jalapeños, or to taste, seeded, ribbed and chopped fine, page 184

2 tablespoons Roasted Garlic Purée, page 88

½ cup coarsely ground Chowder Crackers, or similar, page 175

sea salt, to taste

1 pound smoked whitefish, preferably from Michigan, boned and kept as whole as possible

ACCOMPANIMENTS

Whole Egg Mayonnaise, page 183, following recipe with use of addition of jalapeño peppers

Smoked Whitefish Nachos with White Cheddar, Smoked Tomato Salsa and Jalapeño Cream

Mix the cooked and cooled white beans with the Hickory Smoked Tomato Salsa in a medium non-reactive bowl.

Mound the tortilla chips in a single layer on a heatproof serving platter.

Top with the white bean mixture and dust with half of the white cheddar. Follow with the smoked whitefish and the rest of the white cheddar.

Roast in a preheated 375 degree F oven for 10 to 12 minutes or until the cheese is melted and the dish is warmed through.

Garnish the hot nachos with dollops of the Hickory Smoked Jalapeño Cream, drizzles of both the oils, cilantro sprigs and the lemon and lime wedge.

Serve immediately.

Recommended beverage: Good Harbor M. Foch Rose

Serves 2-4

4 ounces great Northern white beans, cooked and cooled

4 ounces Hickory Smoked Tomato Salsa, page 87

8 ounces freshly fried tortilla chips or similar

4 ounces white cheddar, grated

4 ounces hickory smoked whitefish, preferably from Michigan, flaked

FOR GARNISH
2 ounces Hickory Smoked Jalapeño Cream, page 184

1 ounce Parsley Oil, page 180

1 ounce red chili oil

4 fresh cilantro sprigs

1 lemon wedge

1 lime wedge

Great Lakes Gumbo with White Shrimp and Smoked Whitefish

Serves 6–8

¾ cup soybean oil, preferably from Michigan

¾ cup unbleached all-purpose flour, preferably from Michigan

2 cups red onions, peeled and chopped

1 cup red bell peppers, chopped

1 cup celery, chopped

½ cup Roasted Garlic Purée, page 88

1 tablespoon sea salt, or to taste

1 tablespoon Lake Effect Seasoning, or to taste, page 188

½ teaspoon aji amarillo chili powder, or to taste

5 bay leaves, preferably fresh

1½ quarts Shrimp Stock, page 173

2 pounds white shrimp, preferably from Michigan, or similar, peeled, deveined and butterflied

1 pound smoked whitefish, flaked, preferably from Michigan

½ cup green onions, chopped, reserve a few tablespoons for garnish

½ cup flat leaf parsley, finely chopped, reserve a few tablespoons for garnish

¼ cup filé powder/gumbo file, to taste

½ cup long grain white rice, cooked

½ cup Great Lakes wild rice, cooked

FOR THE ROUX

In a large, heavy cast iron pot, or similar, heat the oil on medium-high heat. When the oil is hot, vigorously whisk in all of the flour. The mixture will eventually smooth out as you whisk and when it reaches the consistency of wet sand it is best to switch from the whisk to a wooden spoon. Slowly continue stirring the roux reaching all over the bottom and corners of the pan. Stir the mixture constantly for 25 to 30 minutes, to achieve a rich dark brown roux or what I like to call 'em— coffee rouz.

FOR THE GUMBO

Add the onions, bell peppers, celery, Roasted Garlic Purée, salt, Lake Effect Seasoning, aji amarillo, and bay leaves to the roux. Cook for 12 to 13 minutes, stirring occasionally until the vegetables are wilted.

Add the stock and mix to blend with the roux. Simmer for 1 to 1½ hours, stirring occasionally and being careful to skim off the foam that will come to the surface.

FOR SERVING

Add the shrimp, smoked whitefish, green onions and parsley and continue cooking for 2 to 3 minutes or until the smoked fish is warmed and the shrimp is just cooked through. Taste and adjust seasonings as necessary.

Ladle the gumbo in a shallow dish. Place a heaping portion of each of the warmed rices in the center of the gumbo. Sprinkle the reserved green onions and parsley over top and serve with the side of filé powder.

Serve immediately.

Recommended beverage: Brys Estate Riesling

unkle e's ramblings
on Gumbo!

Gumbo, the dish is believed to have evolved from the African word for okra, is generally regarded as native to Africa and its westward migration to the new world, and is commonly attributed to the slave trade. In Angola okra is called "ki-ngombo" and you can probably see that in time the "ki" was left behind and ngombo ended up as gombo soon to be what we like to call gumbo. After having said that you probably noticed that there is no okra in my gumbo! hehehe well there is a reason for that, unkle e is not a fan of simmered ki-ngombo — far too "mucilaginous for my taste." But my dear gastronauts, fried okra, well now that's a horse of a different color! Simply season some unbleached all purpose flour with some sea salt and pepper or better yet use my Lake Effect Seasoning (page 188), to taste and dust the okra. Then just heat up some pure Michigan soybean oil to 375 degrees F and fry until crispy. Top the finished gumbo with a nice handful of the fried okra for a great crunchy addition or serve as is for a kewl kocktail treat!

Another classic addition to gumbo is filé powder sometimes called gumbo filé usually ground sassafras root or leaves; filé is used as a thickener as well as flavoring agent. Filé can be an acquired taste and if it's not used as a last minute thickener it can be found sprinkled over the top of gumbo or served on the side.

A classic French thickener, roux is nothing more than fat and flour, usually a 50–50 proposition. Different cooks use varying ratios depending on the dish. The French have but three styles of roux, white, blond and brown. Their culinary cousins in Louisiana have developed a different flavor palette starting with a light brown, medium brown, dark red brown and black. Their dark rich roux mirror their hearty cuisine. In some of the kitchens of New Orleans roux go by the more notorious name of Cajun napalm. These fat and flour slurries are extremely hot and when they splash they stick to your skin causing awful burns so be very careful. What I find most interesting about the roux is that it's not just about thickening especially in Louisiana. The lighter the roux the less flavor but the more thickening power it has. As the color develops the flavor intensifies and consequently the thickening power lessens. This is no doubt one of the reasons why the rich dark gumbos of the crescent city also have okra and filé powder added as flavorful thickeners.

Every major rice producing culture has at least one classic dish based on this versatile grain. The Chinese love it fried and hot, where the Japanese like it cold in sushi or fermented in sake, the Italians revel in creamy risottos, the French produce pounds of pilafs. Right here in the good ol' US of A we have the spiced packed jambalayas of New Orleans, the Carolinas are chock full of pilaus, even out west we have the San Francisco treat, Rice-a-Roni! But one of the first classic recipes I wanted to refresh from a Michigan viewpoint was paella. This

Spanish classic has emerged from its humble origins from the rice producing central plains of Spain as an open air, outdoor picnic food cooked over the occasional log, vine shoots and tree branches. The flames from the hot embers lick the pan and perfume the finished sticky rice with a smoky woodsy flavor. The origins of the dish seemed to have been prepared with whatever was around, broad beans, tomatoes, pork, rabbit and snails all perfumed with saffron and surprisingly enough rosemary.

Michigan Inspired Paella with Rabbit and White Shrimp

In a large, round, shallow, flat pan heat the oil over medium-high heat. Add the strips of pepper and fry until they start to soften.

Sauté the shrimp over medium heat until rare, remove and reserve. Add the rabbit pieces and cook over medium heat until golden brown turning only once, adding more oil, as necessary. Add the paprika, saffron, chopped rosemary, salt and freshly ground pepper.

Push the meat out to the edges of the pan and add the beans and tomatoes in the center, mixing them well.

Add ½ the stock or water making sure to cover the pan until it is ½ full. Simmer for approximately 30 minutes until most of the liquid has evaporated.

Add the rice, distributing it evenly over the pan and fry for a few minutes, moving it around in the pan. Add the rest of the stock/water and cook for about 15 minutes.

Top the paella with the reserved shrimp and gently stir into the rice. Season to taste with more of the salt and freshly ground pepper and cook for another 5 minutes or until the rice is tender and the rabbit is cooked through.

Cover the pan with a clean towel and let it rest for 5 minutes before serving.

Garnish the paella with the sprigs of rosemary and lemon wedges.

Recommended beverage: Brys Estate Riesling

Serves 6–8

2 cups extra virgin cold pressed olive oil

1 whole red bell pepper, cut julienne

2 cups white shrimp, preferably from Michigan, or similar, peeled and deveined

1 whole naturally raised rabbit, preferably from Michigan, cut into pieces

½ teaspoon sweet paprika

1 teaspoon pure saffron, preferably from La Mancha

1 tablespoon fresh rosemary, chopped, with additional sprigs as garnish

½ pound green beans, cut into 1-inch pieces

½ pound broad beans, cut into 1-inch pieces

1 large whole tomato, peeled, seeded and chopped

4½ cups Shrimp Stock, page 173, poultry stock, or water

1¼ pounds short grain rice

lemon wedges, for serving

I'm not sure when I had my first paella but I can say that I couldn't have been more than 8 or 10 when my family vacationed in Madrid. The Villa Magna might have been the most opulent hotel these chubby Bolivian eyeballs had ever seen. From the marbled hallways to the starched linens on the grand dining room tables I was hooked. But it was the paella Valencia that came to our table that really took my breath away. The rice was glistening from its hot bath in Spanish extra virgin olive oil with a warm golden glow courtesy of copious amounts of saffron. Everywhere I looked there was some sea creature bursting from its shell with roasted red peppers and emerald peas along for the ride.

The stinging nettle is a weed that demands to be taken seriously. A member of the nettle family, it can grow up to nine feet in height and has dark green, triangular leaves with toothed edges that grow on opposite sides of the stem. Dare to touch the leaves or stems, which are lined with histamine-packed teeny tiny hairs or trichomes, and you'll end up with a reaction not unlike a chemical burn. I heartily recommend wearing gloves when handling nettles and snipping off the leaves with scissors. Nettles must be cooked to deactivate their sting. Blanched leaves make "way-kewl" wrappers for steamed scallops, shrimp and the like. Boiled nettles can be chopped and added to polenta along with their cooking water to make a tasty, albeit unusual, delightful green porridge.

Stinging Nettle Soup

Serves 4–6

2 tablespoons unsalted sweet butter

2 tablespoons extra virgin cold pressed olive oil

2 whole leeks, trimmed and washed, white and light green parts only, chopped

1 large russet potato, peeled and coarsely chopped

1 large yellow onion, peeled and chopped

2 stalks celery, trimmed and chopped

10 cups (loosely packed) young nettle leaves, washed

2½ cups poultry stock or water

sea salt

Clancy's Fancy Hot Sauce, or similar

½ cup heavy cream, whipped, optional

In a large, heavy non-reactive sauce pot over medium heat, melt the butter and olive oil. Add the leeks, potatoes, onions, celery, and nettles. Cover and cook until vegetables are soft and nettles have cooked down, about 5 to 8 minutes.

Add the stock or water, increase heat to medium-high and bring to a boil. Reduce heat to low and simmer for 20 minutes.

Using an immersion blender purée the mixture until smooth or transfer soup to a blender or food processor and do the same.

Season to taste with the sea salt and hot sauce.

Serve hot, garnished with a dollop of the optional whipped cream.

Quiche Crust

In a large bowl, combine the flour with butter, salt and ½ the water.

Mix lightly with your fingertips until dough forms in pea-sized pieces. You should be able to see chunks of butter, and the dough should be moist enough to begin to stick together. If the dough is too dry, add the remaining water.

Turn the dough out onto a lightly floured work surface, dust with flour, and knead it until the dough is smooth, about 3 to 4 times. Transfer to a plastic bag and form the dough into a disk.

Refrigerate a minimum of 30 minutes, or as long as 3 days.

Makes 2, 8-inch round crusts

3 cups unbleached all-purpose flour

8 ounces unsalted sweet butter

½ teaspoon sea salt

¾ cups ice water

Quiche Custard with Roasted Garlic

In a medium mixing bowl combine the eggs and cream together with a whisk until smooth. Add Roasted Garlic Purée, salt and hot sauce.

Can be refrigerated 2 to 3 days.

Makes 1 pint, good for 1, 8-inch round quiche crust

4 whole eggs

1 cup heavy cream

¼ cup Roasted Garlic Purée, page 88

Clancy's Fancy Hot Sauce, or similar, to taste

sea salt, to taste

Because the baking time of quiche is so short raw vegetables would never have time to cook properly so I have always found it far better to cook the vegetables ahead of time bringing them to their peak flavor and texture potential. This makes a far tastier quiche without the pitfalls of a watery quiche.

Wild Ramp Quiche with Raw Milk Cheddar and Roasted Garlic

Serves 8

3 tablespoons extra virgin cold pressed olive oil

4 cups whole wild ramps, cleaned and chopped

sea salt

black pepper, freshly ground, to taste

1 Quiche Crust, page 27 (½ of recipe)

½ cup raw milk cheddar, or similar, preferably from Michigan, freshly grated

Quiche Custard with Roasted Garlic, page 27

2 tablespoons Parmesan cheese, freshly grated

Preheat the oven to 350 degrees F.

In a preheated sauté pan large enough to hold the ramps add one tablespoon olive oil followed by the ramps. Sauté the ramps over medium heat, seasoning with the salt and pepper for 10 to 15 minutes or until the ramps have nice browned caramelized edges and are tender. Remove from pan and let cool.

Spread the grated cheese evenly over the bottom of the prepared quiche crust and follow with the cooled ramps.

Pour the custard into the quiche shell to within ¼-inch of the top of the crust and scatter the Parmesan over the top. Place the quiche in the middle center of the preheated oven and bake 25 to 30 minutes, or until custard puffs. Allow to cool 10 minutes before serving.

Serve warm or room temperature.

Recommended beverage: Chateau Grand Traverse Reserve Chardonnay

The native Americans knew all about ramps, used in a remedy for coughs and colds, the juice was also transformed into a poultice to sooth the pain and itching of bee stings. CicagaWuni was one name given to the area around the southern shore of lake Michigan where they grew with abandon. Shikako, which loosely translates to "skunk place" referred to the strong smell of these harbingers of spring.

Well, "shikako" is now called Chicago, and the ramp or wild leeks along with the morel are the first seasonal gifts that the mitten offers. "The garlicky onion flavor of Michigan ramps are widely considered to be the sweetest and best of the wild onions," wrote the late great wild food evangelist Euell Gibbons in his epic tome, "*Stalking the Wild Asparagus*." Well, unkle e couldn't agree more!

Fruit Nachos with Murdicks Fudge and Kahlúa Sour Cream

Preheat oven to 375 degrees F.

Mound the tortilla chips in single layer on a heatproof serving platter.

Top the chips with the fruit salad and dust with the grated dark and white chocolate fudge.

Bake in oven for 10 to 12 minutes, or until the fudge is melted and the dish is slightly warmed through.

Garnish with dollops of the Kahlúa Sour Cream, Raspberry Sauce, mint sprigs and powdered sugar.

Serve immediately.

Recommended beverage: Wally's Wineyard Rose

Serves 4-6

6 ounces flour tortilla chips, freshly cooked and seasoned with maple sugar, preferably from Michigan

Michigan Summer Fruit salad, recipe below, drained if necessary

2 ounces Celeste Murdick's Dark Chocolate Fudge, or comparable, frozen and grated

2 ounces Celeste Murdick's White Chocolate Fudge, or comparable, frozen and grated

Kahlúa Sour Cream, page 174

Raspberry Sauce, page 184

fresh mint sprigs, for garnish

powdered sugar, for garnish

Michigan Summer Fruit Salad with Mint and Maple

Place the cubed watermelon in a medium bowl. Trim the strawberries' stems and half or quarter, if large. Cut the peaches into halves and cut into cubes roughly the size of the watermelon and strawberries, add to the bowl of fruit.

Lightly stir the maple syrup and cherry brandy, if using, into the fruit.

Strip the mint leaves off the stem, tear or chop into smaller pieces, and stir into the fruit salad.

Add the berries and set aside for 10 minutes or up to 2 hours.

Serves 4

1 cup watermelon, preferably from Michigan, seeded and cubed

1 cup strawberries

2 Red Haven peaches

3 tablespoons maple syrup, preferably from Michigan

1 tablespoon cherry brandy, or comparable, preferably from Michigan

3-5 sprigs fresh mint

1 cup blueberries, preferably from Michigan

1 cup raspberries, preferably from Michigan

Poached Salmon Fillets with Eggs, Capers and Dill

Serves 4

1½ cups water, or enough to cover the salmon fillets

¾ cup dry white wine, preferably from Michigan

½ whole white onion, peeled and thinly sliced

4 whole hardnecked garlic cloves, skinned and thinly sliced

4 sprigs flat leafed parsley

1 sprig thyme, fresh

four 8-ounce salmon fillets, center cut with the skin

FOR THE SAUCE

2 cups reserved fish poaching broth, strained

½ cup heavy cream

lemon juice, to taste

2 whole eggs, hard-boiled, shelled and chopped

2 tablespoons brined capers, preferably "nonparille," rinsed and chopped

1 tablespoon dill fronds, coarsely chopped

1 tablespoon flat leafed parsley leaves, coarsely chopped

sea salt, to taste

Clancy's Fancy Hot Sauce, to taste

1 tablespoon unsalted sweet butter, cold

Combine the wine, onions, garlic, parsley, thyme and enough water to cover the salmon in wide non-reactive saucepan and bring to a boil for 2 to 3 minutes for flavors to combine.

Season the salmon with the salt and place skin side down in the saucepan and immediately turn the heat down to low. Cover the pan with a parchment paper round, trimmed to fit, and cook until flesh is firm but slightly moist in center about 6 to 8 minutes. Transfer fish to a plate, cover with plastic wrap and reserve in a warm spot.

FOR THE SAUCE

Strain the salmon broth and discard the vegetables. Place the broth back into the saucepan and boil, uncovered, until reduced to about ½ cup (about 5 to 10 minutes). Add the heavy cream and season to taste with the lemon juice. Continue to boil and reduce until thick, about ½ a cup or so. Gently fold in the chopped eggs, chopped capers, dill, herbs and season to taste with the salt and hot sauce. Add the cold butter and shake the pan back and forth to incorporate and create a smooth homogenous sauce. Taste again and adjust seasonings as necessary.

Serve the salmon fillets topped with the hot sauce.

Garnish the finished dish with lemon wedges and any of the herbs that were used in the recipe.

Serve immediately.

Recommended beverage: Shady Lane Pinot Noir

Salmon En Papillote

Preheat the oven to 400 degrees F.

Fold 4 sheets of aluminum (15 x 36-inch) in half like a book. Open the foil on a flat surface to reveal the original sheet, and brush each side with 1 tablespoon of extra virgin cold pressed olive oil.

Generously season the salmon fillets with salt and pepper. In a large mixing bowl add all of the vegetables and season with the salt, pepper, and lemon juice; mix to combine. Divide the vegetables evenly between the four sheets mounding the vegetables in the center of one half of the sheet. Top the vegetables with the salmon fillets and top each fillet with two tablespoons of the compound butter.

At this point you can add the optional mussels (6 per papillote) and divide the fresh breadcrumbs (¼ cup per papillote) by sprinkling over the top.

To close each bag, fold the second side of the paper over the salmon, fold the bottom edge over the top, and work your way edge over edge, folding and twisting, until the bag is sealed.

Place each bag on a baking sheet and bake for about 15 to 20 minutes or until the fish is just cooked through.

To serve, place a bag on each dinner plate and using a paring knife slit each bag in an "X", and fold back the foil (being very careful of the built up steam when you open the pouches).

Serve hot in the foil "papillote" or remove from the foil directly onto the dinner plates.

Recommended beverages: Shady Lane Pinot Noir

Serves 4

4 tablespoons extra virgin cold pressed olive oil

four 8-ounce salmon fillets, Coho, King, etc, skinned

sea salt

black pepper, freshly ground, to taste

¼ cup lemon juice, fresh

1 cup red onions, peeled and cut julienne

1 cup yellow squash, cut julienne

1 cup carrots, peeled and cut julienne

1 cup zucchini, cut julienne

1 cup portabella mushroom caps, cut julienne

1 cup red bell pepper, cut julienne

24 mussels, optional, cleaned and de-bearded

8 tablespoons Compound Butter, page 178

1 cup fresh breadcrumbs, optional

Game Hens On A Grilled Bread Salad with Organic Baby Greens and Horseradish

Serves 2

two 1½ pound Cornish game hens, or similar, brined 12 hours

Basic Maple Brine, page 173

sea salt, to taste

fresh ground pepper, to taste

SALAD AND VINAIGRETTE INGREDIENTS

4 teaspoons white wine vinegar

¼ cup red bell pepper, cut julienne

¼ cup yellow bell pepper, cut julienne

¼ cup red onion, peeled and cut julienne

1 tablespoon prepared horseradish, drained

2 teaspoons Dijon mustard

1 tablespoon Roasted Garlic Purée, page 88

sea salt, to taste

black pepper, freshly ground, to taste

4 scallions, thinly sliced

½ cup extra virgin cold pressed olive oil, plus additional for brushing bread

2 thick slices artisan bread, or similar

3–4 cups organic field greens, preferably from Michigan

The day before you plan to serve the game hens prepare the Basic Maple Brine (optional) and remove neck and giblets from hens and discard. Submerge the game hens in the Basic Brine for up to 12 hours.

In a medium sized mixing bowl combine the white wine vinegar, bell peppers, red onions, horseradish, mustard, Roasted Garlic Purée, salt, pepper, and scallions. Set aside for flavors to meld. Whisk the vinegar and horseradish mixture well and then slowly whisk in all of the olive oil a bit at a time. Taste and adjust seasonings as necessary. Reserve about 3 to 4 tablespoons of the vinaigrette for basting the hens and reserve the rest.

Preheat your gas or charcoal/hardwood grill.

Using a pastry brush liberally coat both sides of the bread with some of the extra olive oil.

Quickly grill the bread on both sides over high heat to achieve strong blackened grill marks but still keeping a moist crumb/center. Remove from the grill and set aside to cool.

Remove the hens from the brine, quickly rinse and pat dry.

Place one hen, breast side down, on cutting board. With kitchen shears or sharp knife, cut along one side of backbone, cutting as close to bone as possible.

Cut down other side of backbone; remove backbone. Spread bird open and turn breast side up, pressing to flatten. Repeat with remaining hen.

To keep drumsticks flat, make small slit through skin with point of knife between thigh and breast. Push end of leg through slit. Repeat on other side of bird and with remaining hen.

Lightly marinate both sides of hens with some of the reserved horseradish marinade and lightly season with sea salt and black pepper.

Place the hens, skin side down, on oiled grill. Grill over medium-high coals 35 to 45 minutes until meat is no longer pink near bone and juices run clear, turning and basting as necessary with reserved horseradish vinaigrette.

Remove the cooked birds from the grill and let them rest (saving any accumulated cooked juices) while you assemble the salad.

In a large mixing bowl tear the cooled grilled bread slices into rough irregular shapes and add to the bowl with the salad greens and any accumulated game hen cooking juices along with the horseradish vinaigrette. Toss well, taste and adjust the seasonings as necessary.

Place the warmed game hens on top of the grilled bread salad and serve immediately.

It has been said that the Rock Cornish game hen was originally bred by Jacques and Alphonsine Makowsky in Connecticut in 1950. By crossbreeding the short-legged, plump-breasted Cornish chicken with various other chickens (including the White Plymouth Rock variety) and game birds, the result was a small bird with all white meat, perfect for a single serving.

Necessity being the mother of invention the Makowsky's originally marketed their baby bird as a temporary substitute for a flock of guinea hens that the farm lost in a fire; it soon became more popular than the guinea hen.

Our U.S. Department of Agriculture requires that all chickens sold as Cornish game hens be no more than 2 pounds in ready-to-cook weight.

Spatchcocking or frogging is the term that is used when small birds such as game hens have the backbone removed and the breast flattened. This allows the bird to be cooked relatively quickly because of its compact shape as well as offering an attractive presentation which also facilitates carving.

Aspen Hill Farms is a family enterprise located in Boyne City Michigan, owned and operated by Steve Edwards. Aspen Hill not only offers naturally raised game hens but rabbits, ducks, cattle, etc.

Hand Rolled Corn Flour Pasta with Golden American Whitefish Caviar, Lemon and Basil

Serves 2 dinner or 4–6 appetizer portions

4 ounces corn flour, organic, preferably from Michigan

6 ounces all-purpose unbleached flour, organic, preferably from Michigan

3 whole large eggs, at room temperature

1 tablespoon extra cold pressed olive oil

¼ cup cornmeal, for dusting the cut pasta

4–5 quarts water

2 tablespoons sea salt

2 tablespoons unsalted sweet butter

½ cup sour cream

4–6 ounces golden American caviar, or similar

2 tablespoons fresh chives, chopped

2 tablespoons fresh lemon juice

BY HAND

Mix and mound the two flours and make a well in the center. Place the eggs and olive oil in the well and, with a fork, slowly begin to beat them. When the eggs are well beaten, start incorporating the flour little by little until the eggs are no longer runny. Bring the mixture together with your hands (leave a tablespoon or two of the flour off to one side — depending on the size of your eggs and the humidity you may not need all the flour). The dough should be on the dry side and not sticking to your fingers. If it is sticky add the remaining flour little by little.

On a clean work surface begin to knead the dough; press on the dough with the palms of your hands and push away from you. Pull it back or fold it and turn the dough clockwise. Knead for about 8 minutes or until the dough is very smooth and silky.

IN A MIXER OR FOOD PROCESSOR

In the mixer or food processor, add the flours (reserving about ¼ cup of blended combination), and then the eggs with the olive oil. Mix until the dough comes together and test by pinching the dough to see if it sticks to your fingers. If it is still sticking add the remaining flour little by little, mixing until it is the right consistency. Finish kneading the last couple of minutes by hand. Wrap the finished dough in plastic wrap and allow to rest for at least one hour.

Cut the dough into 4 pieces and flatten each with the palm of your hand. With either a manual pasta machine or an electric one, start with the widest opening and run each piece of dough through the rollers. Close the opening by one notch and repeat in the same order of running each sheet through the machine. Keep closing the opening by one notch and running the sheets through in the same order until you are down to the last 2 or 3 notches, depending on your machine. Finally using the cutters, cut the pasta into desired width. Lightly dust the cut pasta with cornmeal to help prevent sticking and place on cookie sheets under clean kitchen towels to avoid drying.

In a medium sized sauté pan over medium-low heat melt butter. Add the sour cream, lemon juice, basil and 1 ounce of the caviar. Stir to combine and set aside.

Add the salt to the water and bring to a rapid boil. Gently add the pasta to the boiling water and cook to "al dente" for about 1 minute. Drain the cooked pasta (reserve a bit of the cooking water) and add to the sauté pan. Toss well with the caviar cream. Season to taste with the salt (be careful with the salt, depending on the brand of caviar you are using the salt intensity varies widely) and pepper.

Portion the finished pasta on serving dishes and top each evenly with a bit of sour cream and the remainder of the caviar. Serve immediately.

Great Lakes Vegetable "Fried Rice"

Preheat a wok or large steel pan over high heat until a bead of water vaporizes within one to two seconds of contact.

Swirl in 2 of the 4 tablespoons of the olive oil over high heat and quickly soft-scramble the egg; immediately remove to a plate and reserve.

Swirl in the remaining 2 tablespoons of olive oil into the wok over high heat and stir-fry the ginger, garlic, red onions and scallions for 1 to 2 minutes. Add the bell peppers, asparagus, mushrooms and sweet corn and stir fry for an additional 2 to 4 minutes or until the vegetables are crisp-tender and warmed through.

Add the cooked rice breaking it up with a metal spatula and stir-fry for 2 to 3 minutes or until the rice is coated with the oil and vegetables and warmed through. Add Lemon Vinaigrette and scrambled eggs. Season to taste with the salt and hot sauce.

Mound the finished fried rice on a serving platter and garnish to taste with the sesame oil, rice wine vinegar, sesame seeds and pea shoots.

Serve immediately.

> ⋲ It's preferable to use day old rice so that the drier rice can soak up the flavors.
>
> ⋲ High heat and conservative use of oil makes for a lighter and cleaner dish.
>
> ⋲ Any combination of seasonal vegetables will work well, just keep the sizes similar and look for contrasting textures and colors. Fresh spring peas, fava beans, haricot vert, wild mushrooms are some others that would work well.
>
> ⋲ Use as a base for "Tempura of Fresh Water Perch", or as a stand alone vegetarian entrée.
>
> ⋲ White truffle oil would finish the dish nicely.

Serves 8–10

4 tablespoons extra virgin cold pressed olive oil

1 whole egg, beaten

1 teaspoon fresh ginger, minced

1 teaspoon fresh hardnecked garlic, minced

¼ cup red onions, peeled and cut julienne

¼ cup scallions, chopped white and dark

¼ cup red and yellow bell peppers, cut julienne

6 spears asparagus, blanched and roll cut

6 shiitake mushroom caps, quartered

¼ cup sweet corn kernels, preferably from Michigan, grilled and cut from cob

3 cups long grain white rice, cooked and chilled

1 cup Great Lakes wild rice, cooked and chilled

3 tablespoons Lemon Vinaigrette, or to taste, page 187

sea salt, to taste

Clancy's Fancy Hot Sauce, or similar, to taste

toasted sesame oil, to taste

sushi rice wine vinegar, to taste

sesame seeds black and white, to taste

pea shoots, to taste

Tempura of Yellow Perch

Pour the oil to a depth of at least 3 inches into a deep-fat fryer with a basket or into a deep, heavy pan. If using a deep-fat fryer load the oil per manufacturers directions.

Whenever using a pan for deep frying never fill more than halfway with oil to prevent boil over. Heat to 350 degrees F, checking the temperature on a built-in thermostat or a deep-fat frying thermometer. If you do not have a thermometer, drop in a piece of potato; the oil should immediately begin to foam along its edges.

Dip the fish fillets into the Tempura Batter; shake off any excess and gently add to the oil, taking care not to overcrowd the pan. Fry the fish in batches for approximately 10 to 12 minutes, or until light golden brown. Using tongs gently remove the fish and drain on paper towels.

Season with salt while the fish is still hot.

Serve immediately.

Serves 4

peanut oil, for deep-frying

2 pounds Yellow Perch fillets, preferably from Michigan

Tempura Batter, page 175

sea salt, to taste

Cereal City USA can be found in Battle Creek with the Barrons of Breakfast, Kelloggs and Post Cereals. Both got their start in the late 1800's as health food and now more than 100 years later are more influential than ever.

Michigan's west coast fruit production is sometimes overshadowed by other state icons including Motown's historic auto industry. There can be no dispute however that Michigan at one time was a national powerhouse in fruit production and still remains an incredibly diverse and profitable region. Driving along Lake Michigan's western shoreline takes you through some of the richest farmland on the planet. This narrow swath of culinary real estate hugging the coastline, has been dubbed "Michigan's Fruit Belt," and has lived up to its moniker by producing a dizzying array of fruit including its biggest crops like blueberries, cherries, apples, peaches and strawberries. But we can't forget the grapes, the belt also holds four AVA's or American Viticultural Areas known for the production of quality wine: Fenville, Lake Michigan Shore, Leelanau Peninsula and Old Mission Peninsula. In 2006 there were 1,500 hundred acres under wine-grape cultivation with 45 commercial wineries producing approximately 300,000 cases of wine. A relatively new phenomena is agri-tourism, and combined with wine sales the

The Fruit Belt

industry anticipates sales to reach around 100 million dollars.   While many believed soil to be the reason for the successful growth of our fruit production, others suggested that it was the influence of Lake Michigan. As the spring growing season for grapevines begins, the lakes' cooling effect (stored from the winter) retards the vines from budding until the spring frost season is over. The Great Lakes store daytime heat as the growing season continues. The effect of the warming water lessens the variation between day and night temperatures, which lengthens the growing season (compared to nearby areas) by as much as four weeks. As summer draws to an end, the stored warmth of the lakes delays frost that might damage vineyards in the fall. In winter, the lakes also cause heavy, moist snowfall, which blankets the vineyards, insulating and protecting the vines from the frigid air. The lake effect influences the environment for about 20 to 25 miles inland from the shore, creating a positive viti-cultural environment that wouldn't exist otherwise in the northern climes. It allows Michigan to grow grape varieties that have trouble surviving further south.

Barbecued Pork Shoulder with Maple Apple Rub and Cider Mop

Using a sprinkle jar or by hand lightly dust the entire pork shoulder with half of the rub.

Using a pastry brush give the rubbed pork shoulder a thorough coating of the mustard.

Using the remaining rub dust the entire mustard coated pork shoulder.

Place the drained wood chips in the center of an 18-inch square of heavy-duty aluminum foil. Fold all four sides of foil in to encase the chips creating a "pillow." Repeat the procedure placing the pillow in the center of another square of foil and seal. Turn the double sealed pillow over and with a sharp utility knife cut 4 to 6 holes about the size of a quarter evenly spaced on the surface of the foil to allow the smoke to escape during cooking.

Place the hickory chip pillow on the primary burner of a gas grill. Turn all of the burners to high heat with the lid down and cook until the chips start smoking heavily, about 10 to 20 minutes. Turn the primary burner down to medium-low and turn the rest of the burners off.

Place the seasoned shoulder directly on the grill grate over a disposable foil pan filled halfway with water on the unlit burner and close the lid.

Cook the shoulder for a total of approximately 4 to 6 hours regulating the heat around 250 degrees F. "Mop" the shoulder with the sauce about every 2 hours. The wide variance in traditional barbeque is due in part to the varying size of the pork shoulders, the grill/smoker setup, the fuel, the ambient temperature outside and how you like it cooked.

When the bone easily slides out, the pork is done. Carefully remove the barbecued shoulder from the grill and let it rest for at least 30 minutes covered with foil. Slice shoulder or if you like it shredded leave it in a bit longer and pull pork apart with forks.

Serve the barbeque pork shoulder sliced on a platter with extra mopping sauce on the side or shredded on a bun with the mopping sauce mixed in.

Recommended beverage: Misteguay Hard Apple Cider

Serves 8–10

5–6 pounds Boston butt (bone-in pork shoulder roast), trimmed

1 cup ballpark mustard

Maple Apple Rub, page 46

Barbecue "Mop" with Apple Cider Vinegar, Maple and Jalapeños, page 46

4 cups hickory wood chips, soaked in cold water for 30 minutes and drained

After hundreds of pork shoulders we have found that this rub/mustard/rub method is just a messy proposition but an important one that really gives your barbecue a wonderful flavor and incredible crust. Even though the idea of all that mustard might sound outlandish it's a classic technique used in the French "lapin au moutarde' where rabbit is coated in a thick blanket of Dijon mustard and sautéed.

Barbecue "Mop" with Apple Cider Vinegar, Maple and Jalapeños

Combine all the ingredients in a medium non-reactive saucepan and stir until the maple sugar and salt are dissolved.

Bring to a boil and then reduce heat to medium-low and let simmer for 8 to 10 minutes.

Taste for seasoning, adding salt and sugar as necessary.

Makes 2½ cups

1½ cups raw apple cider vinegar, preferably from Michigan

1 cup fresh apple cider, preferably from Michigan or water

1 tablespoon or more maple sugar, preferably from Michigan

1 tablespoon hot red pepper flakes

1 small red onion, peeled and thinly sliced

1 Hickory Smoked Jalapeño, thinly sliced, page 184, or raw (for a milder sauce, seed the chiles)

2 teaspoons sea salt, or to taste

½ teaspoon black pepper, freshly ground, or to taste

Maple Apple Rub

Combine all the ingredients in a mixing bowl and blend well, use as needed.

Makes about 1½ cups

½ cup sea salt

¼ cup maple sugar, preferably from Michigan

½ cup apple powder

2 tablespoons onion flakes

2 tablespoons roasted garlic powder

1 tablespoon ancho chili powder

1 tablespoon black pepper, freshly ground, or to taste

Can be scaled up or down as needed.

Olive oil can be added to the dry rub to transform it into a wet marinade. Simply whisk in the desired amount of olive oil until a thick paste forms. Use as you would the dry rub for a different effect.

Store the rub in a sealed container preferably away from heat and light in cook dark pantry or freezer. The blend will keep for several months.

Michigan Tart Cherry Worcestershire Sauce

In a large heavy bottomed stockpot over high heat sauté the oil, onions, and jalapeños for 2 to 3 minutes, or until slightly soft.

Add the garlic, pepper, anchovy fillets, cloves, salt, lemons, maple syrup, sorghum, dried cherries, vinegar, water, and horseradish and bring to a boil.

Reduce the heat and simmer, stirring occasionally, for about 6 hours, or until the mixture barely coats a wooden spoon.

Strain into a clean container. Sauce can be refrigerated up to one month.

Makes about 6 cups

¼ cup extra virgin cold pressed olive oil

6 cups red onions, peeled and coarsely chopped

4 whole jalapeños, with stems and seeds, chopped

8 cloves fresh hardnecked garlic, peeled and bruised

2 teaspoons black pepper, freshly ground, or to taste

4 ounces anchovy fillets

½ teaspoon whole cloves

2 tablespoons sea salt

2 medium lemons, skin and pith removed

3 cups maple syrup, preferably from Michigan

1 cup sorghum, preferably from Michigan

6 cups dried tart cherries, chopped

2 quarts apple cider vinegar, preferably from Michigan

4 cups water

2 cups prepared horseradish, drained

It has been said that you don't "pick" morel mushrooms and you don't "gather" them – you "hunt" them. The pursuit may not be a blood sport, but "stalking" better describes what is involved rather than collecting, still the bottom line is – first, you have to find them.

Surprisingly enough, the morel mushroom isn't technically a mushroom at all. The eggheads have said that all mushrooms are fungi and morels are fungi as well, but they do not technically fit the "scientific description" of a mushroom. That "culinary-techno-babel" doesn't stop millions of people all over the world from hunting the elusive "morel mushroom." Considered by many gastronauts to be one of, if not the tastiest of all wild mushrooms the flavor profile is as varied as the hunters who track them. Comparisons to oysters, chicken, sirloin steak and clams have been brought up time and time again but one thing is for sure, they are delicious.

When hunting the morel it's incredibly important on how you store your stash. The late Larry Lonick (aka sporeboy) was a true believer in mesh bags. He felt so strongly that he marketed a waist model that fit like an apron that would not only store the morels but also allow the air to circulate to keep them fresh, as well as allow the morel "spores" to fall back to the forest floor to reseed the species.

Tony Williams, 5 time National morel hunting champion prefers a standard brown paper bag, allowing the morels to stay fresh but more importantly hoards the spores to dust over his own backyard. Marylinn Smith, a Michigan mycologist, has said there is no scientific evidence to support the spore theory and instead prefers a woven basket to hold her prized fungi during the hunt. The rigid woven baskets allow the important airflow needed for freshness but she also feels the rigidity of basket prevents the tender morels from breaking apart. One thing all three agreed on was never ever use plastic bags. Since plastic doesn't breath the morels tend to sweat, dramatically shortening their shelf life. Keep in mind the Michigan season is short, only about 3 to 4 weeks in any one place usually during the month of May depending on weather conditions with the black variety appearing first, followed by the whites and finally the giants. Morels have been such an iconic mitt specialty that festivals have sprouted up to celebrate them. Mesick started their tribute in 1959 with Boyne City quickly following in 1960 and almost fifty years later both festivals are bigger than ever.

Unfortunately because of pollution and urban sprawl some say the wild morel days are numbered, but not Gary Mills and Kris Berglund. Mills holds the patent on the process to grow morels indoors, yes siree I said – indoors! Using local ingredients like sawdust, bark and composted leaves the savvy scientists have set up shop as Woodland Exotics in western Michigan and have been offering the morels and other exotic mushrooms since 2005.

Strozzapreti Pasta with Morel Mushrooms and Asparagus

In a large heavy bottomed non-reactive skillet cook the shallots in the olive oil over medium heat, stirring, until softened. Add the wine, and simmer the mixture until the wine is reduced by half.

Add the Mushroom Broth, Roasted Garlic Purée and morels and simmer the mixture, covered, for 10 minutes, or until the morels are tender.

Add the crème fraîche and the goat cheese and cook the mixture over low heat, stirring, until the cheese is melted. Stir in the asparagus, chives, salt and pepper to taste and keep the sauce warm.

In a large stockpot bring well-salted water to a boil and cook the strozzapreti until it is al dente, drain it well reserving a bit of the cooking water.

Add the drained pasta to the sauce and mix well. If the sauce is too thick add a bit of the reserved cooking water to complete the sauce.

Serve immediately.

Recommended beverage: Shady Lane Semi-dry Riesling

Serves 4

½ cup shallots, peeled and minced

2 tablespoons extra virgin cold pressed olive oil

½ cup dry white wine, preferably from Michigan

½ cup Mushroom Broth, page 172

¼ cup Roasted Garlic Purée, page 88

½ pound fresh morels, washed well, patted dry, and trimmed, preferably from Michigan

½ cup crème fraîche or sour cream

1 cup fresh goat cheese

¾ pound fresh asparagus, trimmed, blanched and cut into 1-inch pieces, preferably from Michigan

¼ cup fresh chives, minced

sea salt, to taste

black pepper, freshly ground, to taste

1 pound strozzapreti or any other thick chewy artisan pasta

Balaton Cherry and Michigan Maple Crisp

Serves 6–8

FOR THE FILLING

3½ pounds fresh Balaton cherries, pitted (You may substitute equal amounts of Bing and Montmorency cherries as an alternative to the Balaton cherries.)

½ teaspoon lemon zest

2 tablespoons "instant" tapioca

¾ cup beet sugar, preferably from Michigan, or similar

2 tablespoons unsalted sweet butter

FOR THE TOPPING

1 cup rolled oats

¾ cup unbleached all-purpose flour, preferably from Michigan

¾ cup maple sugar, preferably from Michigan

1 teaspoon Saigon cinnamon

1 teaspoon sea salt

½ cup unsalted sweet butter, chilled and cut into cubes

Preheat the oven to 375 degrees F.

In a large bowl, mix together the pitted cherries, lemon zest and tapioca.

Gently fold in the sugar to taste.

Grease an 8 x 8-inch or 1½ quart baking dish with butter. Pour the fruit mixture into the dish.

In the bowl of a food processor add the oats, flour, maple sugar, cinnamon and salt.

Pulse for 2 or 3 seconds just to mix.

Add the cold butter cubes and pulse 5 to 10 times or until the butter is just combined.

Sprinkle the topping over the fruit and place in the center of the preheated oven.

Bake for 25 to 35 minutes, or until the topping is golden brown and the fruit is bubbling.

Remove from the oven and cool for 15 minutes before serving.

Recommended beverage: Black Star Farms Cherry Port

Balaton Cherries Jubilee

Serves 4

4 tablespoons unsalted sweet butter

1 pound fresh Balaton cherries, pitted, preferably from Michigan (You may substitute equal amounts of Bing and Montmorency cherries as an alternative to the Balaton cherries.)

¼ cup maple sugar, preferably from Michigan, or less to taste

¼ cup cherry brandy, preferably from Michigan

vanilla ice cream, for serving

OPTIONAL

1 tablespoon "instant" tapioca

1 tablespoon water, cold

In a large, heavy bottomed skillet, melt butter over medium heat. Add cherries and sugar and stir to combine. Cook until cherries are tender and sugar dissolves, about 4 or 5 minutes.

OPTIONAL THICKENER

In a small cup, blend the tapioca and water together, making a slurry. Stir the slurry into the cherry mixture and cook for 1 minute.

Remove skillet from heat. Add brandy and carefully ignite. When flame is extinguished, serve immediately over fresh vanilla ice cream.

Recommended beverage: Chateau Chantal Cherry Sparkling

Cherries on Their Way to Market.
Some of the Million Trees that Abound in the Grand Traverse Region, Traverse City, Mich.

Balaton Cherry Mojo

In a large, heavy bottomed medium saucepan, heat 1 tablespoon of oil over medium-high heat. When the oil is hot, add the shallots, jalapeño and Roasted Garlic Purée.

Cook for five minutes, then deglaze the pan with the cider vinegar, poultry stock and red wine. Cook for three minutes then add the cherries.

Cook for 20 to 30 minutes, or until the mixture has reduced 50 to 70 percent, and/or thickened to a nice sauce-like consistency. Add the parsley. Season with salt, pepper, and hot sauce. Stir in the olive oil. Can be refrigerated 3 to 4 days.

Makes about 1½ cups

1 tablespoon extra virgin cold pressed olive oil

½ cup shallots, peeled and thinly sliced

1 Hickory Smoked Jalapeño, seeded, ribbed and chopped, page 184

1 tablespoon Roasted Garlic Purée, page 88

¼ cup raw apple cider vinegar, preferably from Michigan

2 cups poultry stock

1 cup dry red wine, preferably from Michigan

1 cup fresh Balaton cherries, pitted, preferably from Michigan (You may substitute equal amounts of Bing and Montmorency cherries as an alternative to the Balaton cherries.)

1 tablespoon flat leaf parsley, chopped

sea salt

black pepper, freshly ground, to taste

Clancy's Fancy Hot Sauce, or similar, to taste

1–2 tablespoons extra virgin cold pressed olive oil

Barbecued Pork Ribs with Blueberry Chipotle Chile Rub and Blueberry Mop

Rinse the ribs and blot dry. Remove the thin papery skin on the back of each rack. Pull it off in a sheet with your fingers, using a corner of a dishtowel to gain a secure grip. This allows seasonings to fully penetrate and flavor the pork.

Using a sprinkle jar or by hand heavily coat the pork racks on both sides with the Blueberry Chipotle Chile Rub.

Transfer the ribs to a baking sheet and let cure uncovered in the refrigerator for at least 4 hours or preferably overnight.

Place the drained wood chips in the center of an 18-inch square of heavy-duty aluminum foil. Fold all four sides of foil in, to encase the chips creating a "pillow." Repeat the procedure placing the pillow in the center of another square of foil and seal. Turn the double sealed pillow over and with a sharp utility knife cut 4 to 6 holes about the size of a quarter evenly spaced on the surface of the foil to allow the smoke to escape during cooking.

Place the hickory chip pillow on the primary burner of a gas grill. Turn all of the burners to high heat with the lid down and cook until the chips start smoking heavily, about 10 to 20 minutes. Turn the primary burner down to medium-low and turn the rest of the burners off.

Place the ribs on the grill over a drip pan and cover the grill.

In a small bowl, whisk together all of the ingredients for the mop sauce.

Start basting with mop sauce after 30 minutes, basting every 30 minutes.

Cook the ribs for a total of 4 to 6 hours regulating the heat between 220 and 250 degrees F. The wide variance in cooking times is due in part to the varying size of the pork racks, the grill/smoker setup, the fuel, the ambient temperature outside and how you like it cooked.

The ribs are done when the meat is very tender and it has shrunk back from the ends of the bones.

Carefully remove the ribs from the grill and let it rest for at least 30 minutes loosely covered with foil.

Transfer the ribs to a cutting board or platter. Mop one final time and sprinkle with the remaining rub. Serve immediately.

Recommended beverage: Lake Shore Ruby Red

Serves 4–6

2 racks St. Louis style pork ribs, trimmed

2 cups Blueberry and Chipotle Chile Rub, page 56

FOR THE BLUEBERRY MOP

2 cups raw apple cider vinegar, preferably from Michigan

¼ cup blueberry concentrate, preferably from Michigan

½ cup Dijon mustard

1 tablespoon sea salt

4 cups hickory chips, soaked and drained

Blueberry and Chipotle Chile Rub

Combine all the ingredients in a mixing bowl and blend well.

Makes 1¾ cups

1 cup blueberry powder

1 teaspoon chipotle chile powder

2 tablespoons beet sugar, preferably from Michigan, or similar

2 tablespoons sea salt

1 tablespoon black pepper, freshly ground, or to taste

1 tablespoon smoked paprika

1 tablespoon roasted garlic powder

1 teaspoon dry mustard powder

> Can be scaled up or down as needed.
>
> Olive oil can be added to the dry rub to transform it into a wet marinade. Simply whisk in the desired amount of olive oil until a thick paste forms. Use as you would the dry rub for a different effect.

> Store the rub in a sealed container preferably away from heat and light in cook dark pantry or freezer. The blend will keep for several months.

Roasted Maple Brined Pork Tenderloin with Fresh Blueberries

Serves 4

Basic Maple Brine, page 173

four 8-ounce pork tenderloins, brined and trimmed

1 pint Demi-Glace, page 189

sea salt, to taste

black pepper, freshly ground, to taste

1 cup fresh blueberries

2 ounces Compound Butter, page 178, add lime per recipe instructions

Preheat your oven to 475 degrees F.

Place the brined and seasoned tenderloins in an ovenproof or cast iron pan and place in the center of your hot oven and roast the meat for about 5 to 6 minutes. Then flip meat over and roast until juices run clear. Remove meat from pan and let rest.

In a non-reactive saucepan add the Demi-Glace and season with the salt and pepper. Bring to a boil over medium-high heat and add the blueberries. Bring the sauce back to a boil and let reduce a bit (2 to 3 minutes) so the sauce is thick and the blueberries have burst.

Finish the sauce by adding the Lime Compound Butter and shaking the boiling sauce in the pan to incorporate the butter and emulsify the sauce. Place each tenderloin on a warmed dinner plate and serve with blueberry sauce poured over the top.

Recommended beverage: Shady Lane Pinot Noir

Strawberry Shortcake with Black Walnut Scones

Serves 4–6

FOR THE SCONES

4 cups unbleached bread flour, preferably from Michigan

1⅔ cups unbleached cake flour, preferably from Michigan

3 tablespoons baking powder, plus 1 teaspoon

½ cup beet sugar, preferably from Michigan, or similar

1 cup black walnuts, toasted and chopped, preferably from Michigan

2 teaspoons sea salt

3⅓ cups heavy cream

FOR THE STRAWBERRIES

3 pints fresh strawberries, stemmed, preferably from Michigan

2–3 tablespoons beet sugar, preferably from Michigan, or similar

1 tablespoon fresh lemon juice

2 teaspoons walnut liquor

1 teaspoon fresh lemon zest

FOR THE WHIPPED CREAM

½ cup heavy cream, well chilled

3 tablespoons sour cream

1 tablespoon confectioners' sugar

1–2 teaspoons walnut liquor

FOR THE SCONES
Preheat your oven to 400 degrees F.

In a large mixing bowl add the flours, baking powder, sugar, walnuts and salt. Lightly mix the dry ingredients together with your hands to blend. Add the cream to the blended dry mix and gently mix until incorporated. When the dough holds together turn it out onto a clean, floured work surface and kneed for 1 minute or so until the dough is smooth.

Using a rolling pin gently roll out the dough into a ½-inch thick rectangle. Cut the dough into rounds, squares or whatever shapes you desire being careful not to waste too much dough.

Place the portioned scones onto a prepared cookie sheet lined with parchment paper or silpat sheet. Using a pastry brush, glaze the tops of the scones with a bit of milk for color during baking. Bake the scones in the center of your preheated 400 degree F oven for about 15 minutes or until the scones are golden brown and well risen. Remove to a cooling rack and use as needed.

FOR THE STRAWBERRIES
Rinse and drain strawberries; cut each berry into thick slices or halved and quartered and toss with the sugar in a large mixing bowl. Add the lemon juice, walnut liquor, and lemon zest and gently mix. Set aside.

FOR THE WHIPPED CREAM
In a bowl of a mixer beat the heavy cream with the sour cream and the sugar until it holds a soft shape and beat in the walnut liquor. Refrigerate until needed.

TO SERVE
When ready to serve, split each scone in half horizontally. Place the bottom half on a dessert plate. Spoon about 1 cup of the whipped cream on the scone, arrange a scant cup of strawberries over and around the whipped cream and top with the remaining half of the scone. Add more whipped cream and strawberries if you desire, topping it off with a dollop of whipped cream. Serve immediately.

Recommended beverage: Shady Lane Late Harvest Vignoles

Chilled Raspberry Cream Soup

Serves 4

2 pints fresh raspberries, preferably from Michigan

⅓ cup raspberry dessert wine, or to taste, preferably from Michigan

1 tablespoon beet sugar, preferably from Michigan, or similar, or to taste

sea salt, to taste

1 tablespoon clover honey, preferably from Michigan, or to taste

1 cup heavy cream

2 tablespoons mascarpone cheese

2–4 leaves fresh basil, chiffonade

1 teaspoon Fresh Raspberry Infused Vinegar, recipe below

In the bowl of a food processor or blender place the raspberries, dessert wine, beet sugar, salt and clover honey. Process the berry mixture until you obtain a smooth purée. Add the heavy cream and pulse a few times to blend. It's important that you gently combine the cream so as not to "whip" it.

Taste for seasoning and adjust as necessary.

Strain the mixture through a fine sieve to remove all seeds and refrigerate the soup until needed.

To serve, pour the soup into wide shallow bowls and garnish with the mascarpone, fresh basil and Fresh Raspberry Infused Vinegar.

Fresh Raspberry Infused Vinegar

Makes about 1 cup

½ pint fresh raspberries, preferably from Michigan

½ cup Beet Sugar Simple Syrup, page 186

sea salt

¼ cup champagne vinegar

Place the fresh raspberries, Beet Sugar Simple Syrup and sea salt in a blender or food processor and purée. Add vinegar and taste. Depending on the ripeness of the raspberries the addition of the vinegar is a personal preference kinda thing. Add more vinegar and thin with water if necessary.

Strain through a fine strainer. Can be refrigerated up to 2 weeks.

Roasted Vegetables with Warm Chestnut Vinaigrette

Preheat the oven to 475 degrees F.

Place the vegetables into a large, shallow roasting pan or large baking sheet and toss with the olive oil, salt and pepper.

Roast for 30 to 40 minutes or until tender, stirring occasionally during the cooking time to avoid burning.

Place the hot vegetables on a serving platter topped with the warm Chestnut Vinaigrette.

Serve immediately.

Serves 4

4 parsnips, washed, trimmed and split

4 carrots, washed, trimmed and split

4 beets, washed, trimmed and split

4 baby turnips, washed, trimmed and split

24 spears asparagus, washed and trimmed

2 whole red onions, peeled and quartered

4-5 tablespoons extra virgin cold pressed olive oil

sea salt, to taste

black pepper, freshly ground, to taste

1 cup Warm Chestnut Vinaigrette, recipe below

Warm Chestnut Vinaigrette

Combine all the ingredients for the vinaigrette in a non-reactive medium saucepan.

Heat over low heat until warm.

Whisk the vinaigrette well, use immediately.

Makes about 1⅓ cups

½ cup extra virgin cold pressed olive oil

½ cup walnut oil

⅓ cup sherry wine vinegar

1 tablespoon water

sea salt, to taste

black pepper, freshly ground, to taste

12 Roasted Chestnuts, page 174, preferably from Michigan or similar, peeled and roughly chopped

Sugar Baked Pear Pizza with Maytag Blue Cheese, Arugula and Toasted Walnuts

Place a pizza stone on the middle rack of the oven and preheat the oven to 500 degrees F.

On a lightly floured surface, stretch or roll out the Michigan Maple Pizza Dough into an 8 to 10-inch circle, with the outer edge a little thicker than the inner circle.

Brush the dough with the vinaigrette and top with the arugula, pear slices, blue cheese, and walnuts.

Drizzle a bit more of the vinaigrette and dust with the Parmesan.

Slide a pizza paddle or rimless baking sheet under the pizza and then slide the pizza onto the pizza stone. Bake until the crust is golden brown, 6 to 8 minutes.

With the pizza paddle or a large spatula, carefully remove the pizza from the oven and set it on a cutting board.

Using a pizza cutter or a large sharp knife, cut the pizza into 4, 6 or 8 slices.

Serve immediately.

Makes one, 8-inch pizza

1 ball Michigan Maple Pizza Dough, page 156

2 tablespoons Red Onion Walnut Vinaigrette, page 177

¼ cup arugula, cleaned

½ Sugar Baked Pear, page 63, sliced

2 tablespoons Maytag Blue cheese, or similar, crumbled

1 tablespoon walnuts, toasted and chopped

1 tablespoon Wisantigo Parmesan, or similar, grated

Sugar Baked Pears

Preheat your oven to 300 degrees F.

Line a suitable size cookie sheet or small roasting pan with parchment paper. Add the sugar to sheet or pan and spread out to cover about ¼ of an inch.

Rub the cut sides of each of the pear halves with a bit of the salt and place cut side onto the sugar and bake for one hour.

After cooking let the pears cool to room temperature. When cool enough to handle gently remove the core and stem from the fruit.

Can be refrigerated 3 to 5 days.

Recommended beverage: Black Star Farms Sirius Pear Dessert Wine

Serves 4

1 cup beet sugar, preferably from Michigan, or similar

4 whole pears, preferably from Michigan, cut in half, stem to core

1 tablespoon sea salt

Grilled Bananas with Michigan Hard Apple Cider Glaze

Serves 4

FOR THE GLAZE

¼ cup hard apple cider, preferably from Michigan

¼ cup Apple Cider Syrup, also known as boiled cider, recipe below

¼ cup unsalted sweet butter

1 whole lime, juiced

4 large bananas, unpeeled and halved lengthwise

3 tablespoons soybean oil, preferably from Michigan

1 pint vanilla ice cream, preferably from Michigan

Combine first 4 ingredients for the cider glaze in a non-reactive saucepan and bring to a boil. Reduce heat to low and simmer until the mixture is smooth and thick about 2 to 3 minutes. Remove from heat and reserve.

Rub the banana halves lightly with the oil and place cut side down on the grill over medium heat for 1 to 2 minutes or until the bananas are just golden brown.

Turn the bananas over (skin side down) and immediately paint the grilled surface with the glaze and cook about 1 to 2 minutes more.

To serve, place two hot banana halves skin side down on a plate along with a scoop of ice cream and finish with a drizzle of the hard cider glaze, serve immediately.

Recommended beverage: Grand Traverse Select Sweet Harvest Reisling

Apple Cider Syrup/Boiled Cider

Makes about 2 cups

1 gallon fresh apple cider, preferably from Michigan and unpasturized

In a large, heavy bottomed non-reactive stockpot over high heat bring the cider to a boil. Reduce heat to medium-high and let the cider reduce to one pint. Be careful when you get close to the end, as it reduces it thickens and begins to foam up, which makes it difficult to determine what is left in the pot. Take care that the pot is big enough so you don't experience a boil over. Let cool and use as needed.

The New England colonists used apple cider syrup or boiled cider as a sweetener for baking and flavoring. It's a dark brown syrup with an intense apple flavor and a surprising snap to the taste, which balances the sweetness. I like using it as is, drizzled over roasted poultry or pork as well as the base of a glaze, marinade or barbecue sauce.

Grilled Grape Leaves Stuffed with Goat Cheese and Dried Tart Cherries

Serves 4

8 ounces fresh goat cheese, preferably from Michigan

½ teaspoon sea salt

⅛ teaspoon black pepper, freshly ground, or to taste

3 tablespoons extra virgin cold pressed olive oil

1 tablespoon lemon juice

8 large grape leaves, packed in brine and rinsed

½ cup dried tart cherries, preferably from Michigan

2 cups extra virgin cold pressed olive oil

8 thick slices artisan bread

Turn grill to high flame.

Mix goat cheese with the lemon juice, sea salt, black pepper, lemon juice and 3 tablespoons of extra virgin cold pressed olive oil in a medium mixing bowl, set aside.

Spread out grape leaves in sets of two overlapping leaves.

Scoop about two ounces—a rounded heaping tablespoon—of goat cheese mixture and place it in the middle of a pair of grape leaves.

Push 4 or 5 dried tart Michigan cherries in the center of the cheese.

Starting with one end, fold each side of the leaf pair until goat cheese is covered, making a rounded packet.

Repeat with remaining leaves.

Place stuffed leaves in a shallow dish and cover with extra virgin olive oil until ready to cook.

Using tongs, place the packets onto the grill folded side down. When marked on one side, about one minute, turn over and grill until marked on the other side.

When cheese is soft (about one more minute) remove packets from grill and place on platter.

Brush slices of bread with olive oil, season with salt and pepper and grill both sides until lightly browned and toasted.

Remove from grill and serve with the grilled grape leaves.

Recommended beverage: Chateau Grand Traverse Johannisberg Reisling

Rack of Baby Lamb with Prunes, Apricots and Dried Cherries

Preheat the oven to 400 degrees F.

Season the fat on the meaty sides of each rack with the sea salt and black pepper and rub with olive oil.

Place the lamb on a roasting pan meaty-side up, and cover the bones with aluminum foil to prevent them from burning as they cook. Roast the racks of lamb 20 to 25 minutes for medium-rare. While the racks are roasting, make the sauce.

In a medium skillet or saucepan heat the butter over medium-high heat. When the butter is foaming add the onions, celery, and shallots.

Season to taste with the salt and pepper, cook, stirring, for 1 minute. Add the Roasted Garlic Purée, apricots, cherries, and prunes, and cook for 2 minutes. Add the port, red wine and stock to the pan and cook until the liquid has reduced down about 70 percent, around 25 to 30 minutes. At this point add the mint and walnuts, and stir well to combine. Season again to taste with the salt and black pepper.

Swirl the cold butter into the sauce off the heat, and serve immediately over the lamb.

Recommended beverage: Black Star Farms Red House Red

Serves 4

4 full racks baby lamb, about 1 pound each, trimmed

1 teaspoon sea salt, or to taste

1 teaspoon black pepper, freshly ground, or to taste

2 tablespoons extra virgin cold pressed olive oil

FOR THE SAUCE

1 tablespoon unsalted sweet butter

¼ cup red onions, peeled and finely chopped

2 tablespoons celery, chopped

1 tablespoon shallots, peeled and minced

sea salt

black pepper, freshly ground

1 tablespoon Roasted Garlic Purée, page 88

¼ cup dried apricots, finely chopped

¼ cup dried tart cherries

¼ cup prunes (dried plums), finely chopped

1 cup port wine

¾ cup red wine

2 cups lamb, chicken or veal stock

1 tablespoon fresh mint leaves, chopped

¼ cup walnuts, toasted and chopped

3 tablespoons unsalted sweet butter, chilled

Maple Planked Breast of Chicken with Tomato Horseradish Rub and Mixed Vegetables

Serves 2

two 8–10 ounce breasts of chicken, boneless, with the skin, preferably from Michigan

2 large untreated maple cooking planks

4 tablespoons Tomato Horseradish Rub, page 69

5 tablespoons extra virgin cold pressed olive oil

4–5 cups water

1–2 whole red skin potatoes, cooked, cooled and cut in half

1 whole portabella mushroom cap, stemmed and cut in half

1 whole red bell pepper, quartered and cored

1 whole yellow bell pepper, quartered and cored

1 whole red onion, peeled and quartered

1 whole Roma tomato, cored and cut in half

2 sprigs fresh rosemary

1 whole lemon, split in half, stem to core, juice one half, reserve other for garnish

sea salt, to taste

black pepper, freshly ground, to taste

Mix 2 tablespoons of the rub with 2 tablespoons of the olive oil until well blended. Coat each chicken breast thoroughly with the paste. Cover and place in the refrigerator at least 30 minutes or overnight.

Preheat the oven to 400 degrees F.

Place the planks inside suitable baking sheet/pan that will hold the plank and pour the water around the plank to come up about halfway.

In a mixing bowl, toss the mixed vegetables with the lemon juice and remaining olive oil. Season with the rub, one of the rosemary sprigs and additional salt and black pepper if needed. Toss until well mixed.

Place the planks with the vegetables in the hot oven, in the center and let roast for 10–12 minutes.

Carefully remove the pan from the oven and place the seasoned chicken breast skin side up with the cooking vegetables.

Return the plank to the oven and roast for another 15 to 18 minutes or until the juices in the chicken breast run clear.

Carefully remove the plank from the oven and garnish with the remaining lemon half, quartered and the second rosemary sprig.

Serve immediately on the plank.

Recommended beverage: Bel Lago Pinot Grigio/Chardonnay

With the long cooking time you will probably notice the plank begin to warp. Not to worry. After you are done simply wash and dry thoroughly. For storage, invert the plank and after a while the plank will straighten itself out. Alternatively, if you are using a two sided plank, follow the same procedure but alternate sides when cooking.

Tomato Horseradish Rub

Combine all ingredients in small bowl.

Store the rub in a sealed container preferably away from heat and light in cool, dark pantry or freezer. The blend will keep for several months.

Makes about 1½ cups

4 tablespoons tomato powder

2 tablespoons ancho chili powder

2 tablespoons horseradish powder

2 tablespoons fresh lemon zest

4 tablespoons lavender

4 tablespoons roasted garlic powder

8 teaspoons sea salt

⊨ Can be scaled up or down as needed.

⊨ Use for poultry, fish and vegetables.

⊨ Olive oil can be added to the dry rub to transform it into a wet marinade. Simply whisk in the desired amount of olive oil until a thick paste forms. Use as you would the dry rub for a different effect.

Maple Planked Camembert with Mixed Dried Fruits

Serves 2–4

1 tablespoon dried cranberries, preferably from Michigan

1 tablespoon dried blueberries, preferably from Michigan

1 tablespoon dried tart cherries, preferably from Michigan

½ cup hard apple cider, preferably from Michigan

1 large untreated maple cooking plank or shingle

1 8-ounce Camembert cheese wheel, preferably from Michigan, under-ripe preferred

2 tablespoons walnuts, toasted and chopped

1½ teaspoons maple sugar, preferably from Michigan

1 whole Honeycrisp apple, preferably from Michigan, or similar, cored and quartered into wedges

1 ounce walnut oil

1 loaf artisan bread, sliced

Preheat your oven to 400 degrees F.

In a small non-reactive pan add the dried fruits and the hard cider. Bring to a boil and reduce until the fruit has plumped and the cider is syrupy, about 3 to 5 minutes. Remove from heat and let cool.

Place the hardwood plank in the center of the preheated oven for 10 to 12 minutes.

While the plank is heating, cut the rind from the top of the cheese and cover with the cooled fruit mixture. Follow with the chopped walnuts and sprinkle over the maple sugar.

When the plank is hot carefully remove from the oven and place the fruit and nut topped cheese on the center of the hot hardwood plank. Carefully place the apple wedges (skin side in) against the cheese sides to prevent oozing. Place into the oven and let cook for 10 to 12 minutes or until the cheese is warmed through.

Remove the cheese from the oven and serve on the warmed plank. Drizzle the walnut oil over the cheese and serve with the bread.

—€ Even though cheeses are best eaten at their peak of ripeness, baked Camembert and Brie are preferable when they are well refrigerated and firm or a bit under-ripe. Since the baking causes the cheese to melt, the firm, under ripe cheese actually works better since it stays firmer longer, allowing the flavors to develop and the nuts and sugar to caramelize. So, a basic rule of thumb is, the firmer (under-ripe) the cheese the longer the cooking time and the riper (softer) the cheese the shorter the cooking time.

—€ The apple slices are like culinary architecture in that they help keep the cheese intact during cooking — and you get to eat 'em!

—€ If hard cider is unavailable or not part of your diet, regular cider or apple juice, cranberry juice etc. would work just fine.

Spit Roasted Whole Pineapple with Dried Cranberries and Lemon

In a small, non-reactive saucepan combine the clover honey, cranberries, black pepper, lemon juice and fresh mint. Cook over medium heat, stirring occasionally until just warmed through and syrupy, about 3 to 5 minutes. Remove from heat and reserve.

Trim the skin of the pineapple being careful not to remove the stalk. Cover the stalk with aluminum foil to prevent burning the leaves. Rub the entire flesh of the pineapple with the olive oil and place on the rotisserie according to the manufacturers directions. Cook the pineapple about one hour or until the pineapple is warmed through, basting with the Lemon Honey Glaze every 15 minutes.

If using the whole pineapple, carve the "fruit roast" like a loaf of bread and reconstruct the roasted sliced pineapple on a platter with the stalk at the top. Pour over the remainder of the glaze over the grilled pineapple and serve immediately.

Alternatively, peel and slice the pineapple into 1-inch thick, round slices. Rub both sides of the cut pineapple with the olive oil and place on a grill over a medium fire and cook on both sides for about 2 to 4 minutes or until lightly charred and heated through. During the last minute or so of cooking brush the pineapple slices with the Lemon Honey Glaze and remove to a serving platter, and pour the the remainder of the glaze over the grilled pineapple and serve immediately.

Recommended beverage: Leelanau Apricot Wine

Serves 6–8

FOR THE LEMON HONEY GLAZE

½ cup clover honey, preferably from Michigan

6 tablespoons dried cranberries, preferably from Michigan

1½ teaspoons black pepper, freshly ground

4 whole lemons, juiced

½ cup fresh mint, chopped

1 large pineapple, with the stalk attached

2–3 tablespoons extra virgin cold pressed olive oil

Kids, this is an antioxidant powerhouse of a beverage! Michigan Blueberries are behemoths in the health food world, packed full of vitamin C, fiber, along with other elements that have been proven to prevent many common diseases. So drink it up, it's a longevity-enhancing beverage that tastes wonderful as well.

One pound of carrots will make approximately six to eight ounces of carrot juice.

Drink juice immediately or within a few days. Carrot juice does not keep for long and tastes best when fresh.

Carrot Blueberry Juice

Serves 1

6 fresh carrots, preferably from Michigan

1 handful of fresh blueberries, preferably from Michigan

12 tablespoons fresh lime juice

Using a masticating juicer or similar, alternate between the carrots and the blueberries as you run them through the machine. Add a slight amount of water to the discarded pulp and rerun through the machine to completely extract all of the juice.

Stir in the lime juice and serve with ice cubes.

Carrot Watermelon Juice

Serves 1

6 fresh carrots, preferably from Michigan

1 quarter of a medium watermelon, preferably from Michigan

Using a masticating juicer or similar, alternate between the carrots and the watermelon (rinds and seeds too!) as you run them through the machine. Add a slight amount of water to the discarded pulp and rerun through the machine to completely extract all of the juice.

Serve with ice cubes.

Carrot Peach Juice

Serves 1

6 fresh carrots, washed, preferably from Michigan

2 Red Haven peaches, skin and pit removed, preferably from Michigan

Using a masticating juicer or similar, alternate between the carrots and the peaches as you run them through the machine. Add a slight amount of water to the discarded pulp and rerun through the machine to completely extract all of the juice.

Serve with ice cubes.

The masticating juicer is an odd looking beast; it chews it's food rather than squeezes it, then discards the abused pulp giving you more fiber, enzymes, vitamins and trace minerals. This all results in the darker, richer color of the juice and a sweeter, richer more full-bodied flavor.

Double Blueberry Lime Ice Cream

In a non-reactive saucepan, heat the blueberries and ¼ cup of the beet sugar over medium heat, stirring occasionally, until the berries pop and begin to cook down, about 10 minutes. Set aside to cool, then refrigerate until ready to use.

In a medium, heavy bottomed non-reactive saucepan, heat the cream, half and half, vanilla extract and blueberry concentrate over medium heat, stirring occasionally to make sure the mixture does not burn or scorch on the bottom. When it reaches a simmer (do not let it boil), turn off the heat and set aside to infuse 10 to 15 minutes.

In a medium bowl, whisk together the egg yolks and the remaining ¾-cup beet sugar. Whisking constantly, slowly pour the still hot cream mixture into the egg yolk mixture (this technique is called tempering the eggs).

Return the mixture to the saucepan and cook over medium heat, stirring constantly with a wooden spoon or heatproof rubber spatula. When the custard reaches 180 degrees F it should be thick and creamy; quickly remove it from the heat.

If you have time this could be done the day before to properly chill. If you don't have the time fill a large bowl halfway with ice water. Strain the mixture into a smaller bowl and whisk in the lime juice and lime zest. Rest the smaller bowl in the ice water and let the mixture cool, stirring often, then continue according to the directions of your ice cream maker.

When the ice cream base is finished, transfer to a large mixing bowl and using a sturdy rubber spatula, fold in the blueberry mixture until swirled. Freeze for at least 4 hours to harden and cure.

Makes about 1 quart

1 cup blueberries, fresh, preferably from Michigan

1 cup beet sugar, preferably from Michigan, or similar

2 cups heavy cream

2 cups half and half

½ teaspoon pure vanilla extract

2 tablespoons blueberry concentrate, preferably from Michigan

9 egg yolks

2 whole limes, juiced

1 tablespoon lime zest, freshly grated

Double Apple Galette

Serves 8

½ of 1 recipe Apple Pâte Brisée, page 181

5 large apples, seasonal antique varieties, preferably from Michigan

¼ cup beet sugar, preferably from Michigan, or similar

3 tablespoons unsalted sweet butter, cut into small pieces

1 small whole lemon, juiced

4 tablespoons apricot preserves

1 tablespoon apple brandy, optional, preferably from Michigan

Make one recipe of the Apple Pâte Brisée. Use half for one galette and wrap the remainder and reserve for a later use. Roll out the dough ⅛ to ¹⁄₁₆-inch thick, in a shape that fits roughly on a cookie sheet or approximately 16 x 14-inches.

Peel and cut the apples in half, core them, and slice each half into ¼-inch slices. Set aside the large center slices of the same size and chop the end slices coarsely.

Sprinkle the chopped apple over the center of the dough. Arrange the large slices on the dough beginning at the outside, approximately 1½ inches from the edge. Stagger and overlap the slices as you go.

Cover the dough completely with a single layer of apples, except for the border. Bring up the border of the dough and fold it over the apples. Sprinkle the apples with the beet sugar and spot with the pieces of butter. Finally squeeze the fresh lemon juice over all and bake in a 400 degree F oven for 65 to 75 minutes, until the crust is really well browned and crusty like a pizza.

Slide it onto a board. Warm the apricot preserves with the apple brandy (or use 1 tablespoon of water if the jam is thick and you prefer not to use alcohol) and spread it on top of the apples with a pastry brush or back of a spoon.

It's best to serve the galette at room temperature, cut into wedges.

Recommended beverage: Shady Lane Sparkling Riesling

Traditionally a galette is free form and resembles a pizza more than a tart with its thin and large crust. Also in the European manner this dessert is at its best when it's served warm or at the least, room temperature.

Honeycrisp is the new sensation in the apple world, a large, sweet fruit with crisp "to-die-for" texture! The University of Minnesota breeders at Excelsior, MN introduced an offspring of macoun and honey gold, the Honey-crisp in 1991. As you can imagine by the name, this apple has a bright sweet flavor but the real kicker in Honeycrisp is its explosively crisp texture. I can't think of another apple that matches its crispness.

Do not worry about the discoloration of the apples after you peel and arrange them on the dough. The discoloration will not be apparent after cooking.

The palm or Middle of the Mitt might not be as sexy as other parts of the state, but it's no less important. In our travels, the Middle of the Mitt begins at Motown, better known as Detroit. Here you will find the classic Coney dog in two basic varieties: the Detroit style, which is loose and chili-like with tomatoes and beans, contrasting with the Flint style which is considerably drier and bean-less. The wiener of choice in either instance is the naturally-cased Vienna variety made near Flint by Koegel meats. ⬜ Another Detroit icon, Henry Ford, is said to have used soybeans to produce an auto trunk lid. Over 10,000 Middle of the Mitt farmers grow nearly 75 million bushels of this miracle crop yearly which can be found in everything from printing ink and biofuels to baby formulas and salad dressings. ⬜ Moving northwest you will find the sleepy town of Potterville.

Middle *of the* Mitt

With a population of just over 2,100 people the rural downtown swells to an astonishing 16,000 souls for the annual Gizzard Fest, home of the now classic chicken gizzard-eating contest. Joe's Gizzard City batters and deep-fries these provocative poultry parts offer you an afternoon you won't soon forget — even if you want to! ▢ Head over to I-75 north and in a few hours you'll be starring at the Mackinaw Bridge, the third largest suspension bridge in the USA. Since Michiganders residing in the U.P. are called "Yoopers" it only seems right that the downstaters have nicknames too. "Fudgies" categorize the chocolate chopping tourists of the northern coast, but a more general name for everybody under the bridge is "troll." I kinda like the idea of being called a troll especially if the bridge we are talking about is the Mighty Mac.

Bolivian Macaroni and Cheese

Serves 10–12

2–3 tablespoons unsalted sweet butter, softened

FOR THE BREADCRUMBS

2 tablespoons unsalted sweet butter

6 slices artisan bread, lightly pulsed in a food processor or run against a cheese grater

sea salt, to taste

black pepper, freshly ground, to taste or ancho chili powder, to taste

FOR THE BEURRE MANIÉ

½ cup unbleached all-purpose flour

6 tablespoons unsalted sweet butter

FOR THE ROASTED GARLIC BÉCHAMEL

5½ cups whole milk

2–3 teaspoons sea salt, or to taste

¼ teaspoon nutmeg, freshly grated

¼ teaspoon black pepper, freshly ground

4–6 bay leaves, whole

¼ teaspoon aji amarillo or ancho chili powder, or to taste

¾ cup Roasted Garlic Purée, page 88

TO FINISH THE MACARONI AND CHEESE

2 cups provolone, grated

2½ cups fresh cow's milk mozzarella, grated

1¼ cups Wisantigo Parmesan, or similar, grated

1 pound penne pasta

sea salt, to taste

Preheat your oven to 375 degrees F.

Butter the 3-quart casserole dish (or similar heatproof dish) with the softened unsalted butter, set aside.

FOR THE BREADCRUMB TOPPING

Place the fresh breadcrumbs in a medium bowl. In a small saucepan over medium heat, melt 2 tablespoons butter. Add the butter to the breadcrumbs, season with the salt, pepper and chili powder and toss to coat. Set breadcrumbs aside.

FOR THE BEURRE MANIÉ

In a medium bowl knead the remaining 6 tablespoons butter with your fingers with the half-cup of flour until well blended. You're going to end up with a doughy-like mass, this is what you want—trust unkle e!, reserve.

FOR THE ROASTED GARLIC BÉCHAMEL

In a large, heavy bottomed saucepan set over medium heat, bring the milk, salt, nutmeg, black pepper, bay leaves, chili powder and Roasted Garlic Purée to a simmer, whisking all the time, for about 5 minutes. Remove the pan from the heat and let the mixture steep for 20 minutes to allow the flavors to bloom and meld.

Put the pan back on the heat and bring to a boil while whisking and gently crumble in the Beurre Manié. Continue cooking, whisking vigorously and constantly, until the mixture bubbles and becomes thick. Let the mixture gently simmer for about 5 to 10 minutes for flavors to blend, and the raw flour flavor to cook out a bit.

TO FINISH THE BOLIVIAN MACARONI AND CHEESE

Remove the pan from heat and stir in 1 of the 2½ cups of mozzarella cheese, 1 of the 2 cups provolone and 1 of the 1¼ cups Wisantigo Parmesan to the Roasted Garlic Béchamel to blend. Set the sauce aside.

Fill a large saucepan with water, add salt to taste and bring to a boil. Cook the pasta 2 to 3 minutes less than manufacturer's directions, until the outside of the pasta is cooked and the inside is just a bit underdone.

Drain the pasta and add to the reserved sauce. If the saucepan is not big enough to accommodate both the pasta and the sauce transfer to a suitable mixing bowl.

Pour mixture into the buttered casserole. Sprinkle remaining 1½ cups mozzarella, 1 cup provolone, ¼ cup of the Wisantigo Parmesan, and breadcrumbs over top.

Bake until browned on top, about 30 minutes. Transfer dish to a wire rack to cool slightly, about 5 minutes. Serve hot.

Recommended beverage: Good Harbor Trillium

Quesadilla of Huitlacoche with White Cheddar Cheese

Serves 4

3 tablespoons extra virgin cold pressed olive oil

1 small red onion, peeled and finely chopped

1 whole smoked jalapeño, seeded and minced

1 large ripe tomato, diced

1 tablespoon Roasted Garlic Purée, page 88

1½ pounds fresh huitlacoche, preferably from Michigan or canned

2 tablespoons fresh cilantro, chopped

sea salt, to taste

black pepper, freshly ground, to taste

1 cup white cheddar cheese, grated

4 large flour tortillas

FOR GARNISH

¼ cup Hickory Smoked Tomato Salsa, page 87

¼ cup Hickory Smoked Jalapeño Cream, page 184

8 sprigs fresh cilantro

1 whole lime, cut into eighths

In a large, heavy bottomed skillet heat the oil over medium heat.

Add the onions and jalapeños and sauté for 3 to 5 minutes or until limp. Add the tomato and Roasted Garlic Purée and cook for another minute or so. Add the huitlacoche and stir breaking up the corn smut with a wooden spoon. Cover the skillet and cook for 10 to 15 minutes or until the mixture is thick and creamy.

Stir in the cilantro and season with the salt and pepper and cook for another minute or so. Remove from heat and reserve. This base can be made up to 4 days in advance.

FOR QUESADILLAS

Spoon the huitlacoche and white cheddar equally between the flour tortillas on one side. Fold the opposite side over the filling to create a half moon.

Place the quesadillas on an oiled cookie sheet and bake in a 350 degree F oven for 10 to 20 minutes or until the filling is warmed and cheese is melted.

Serve hot with the optional Hickory Smoked Tomato Salsa, Hickory Smoked Jalapeño Cream, cilantro and lime wedges.

Recommended beverage: New Holland Brewing Oatmeal Stout

unkle e's ramblings on corn smut!

You wanna talk smut? Do yah? Well, let's get into it then — the Mexican huitlacoche (wheet-lah-KOH-chay) or corn smut as they say here in the ole U.S. of A. is one of those bizarre culinary mysteries. While some cultures regard it as a plague and throw it away, others prize it as one of the planet's most tasty albeit unusual culinary delicacies. Often referred to as the "Mexican truffle" huitlacoche is a mushroomy flavored fungus that grows on ears of corn during unusual seasonal conditions. Michigan weather unusual? shuutup! It is said that the Aztecs adored the "black pudding" for its smoky sweet flavor and creamy texture. Well, when my pal Susan at Giving Tree Farm in Lansing mentioned she had some — hell you all know me by now, I had to have it too! Do try my Quesadilla stuffed with huitlacoche and dine like an Aztec god!

Grilled Lamb with Mint Horseradish Glaze on Warm White Bean Salad

FOR THE GLAZE
Whisk ingredients together in a medium bowl and season with salt and pepper to taste, reserve.

FOR THE LAMB
Preheat grill to high. Brush loins on both sides with olive oil and season with salt and pepper. Grill for 2 to 3 minutes on both sides for medium-rare doneness or until the internal temperature reaches 140 to 145 degrees F. Remove from grill and brush with a few tablespoons of the glaze reserving the rest for the salad.

FOR THE SALAD
In a medium sauté pan over a medium-high heat add the olive oil and the onions and sauté for 2 to 3 minutes or until the onions are limp. Follow with the white beans, artichoke hearts, tomatoes and mint.

Heat the mixed vegetables until warmed and taste for seasonings. Remove from heat and let cool slightly.

Thin out the remaining glaze to taste with the lime juice and olive oil.

In a medium bowl toss the baby greens with the slightly cooled bean mixture and dress to taste with the thinned out glaze. Immediately place on a serving plate and top with the rested lamb loins.

Recommended beverage: Peninsula Cellars Cabernet/Merlot

Serves 2

FOR THE GLAZE

¼ cup Dijon mustard

2–3 tablespoons clover honey

2 tablespoons prepared horseradish, drained

¼ cup fresh mint, chopped

2–3 tablespoons lime juice

sea salt, to taste

black pepper, freshly ground, to taste

FOR THE LAMB

2 whole boneless lamb loins

1–2 tablespoons extra virgin cold pressed olive oil

sea salt, to taste

black pepper, freshly ground, to taste

FOR THE SALAD

2 tablespoons extra virgin cold pressed olive oil

½ medium red onion, peeled and cut julienne

1 cup great Northern white beans, cooked and drained

½ cup canned artichoke hearts, drained and rinsed well

1 large ripe tomato, cut into eighths

¼ cup mint, stemmed and chiffonade

2 cups baby mixed greens, loosely packed

2 tablespoons extra virgin cold pressed olive oil

2 tablespoons lime juice

Hickory Smoked Tomato Salsa

Gently skin the smoked tomatoes using your thumb and index finger. Cut the tomatoes across the equator and gently squeeze to extract the seeds. Cut the skinned and seeded tomato halves into ¼-inch dice and transfer to a bowl with any accumulated juices.

Wearing rubber gloves, stem, seed, rib and finely chop the smoked jalapeño chiles.

In a medium mixing bowl add the tomatoes, jalapeños, onions, cilantro, Roasted Garlic Purée, olive oil and lime juice; mix thoroughly. Season to taste with the salt, pepper, and hot sauce.

Can be refrigerated 3 to 5 days.

Makes about 1 quart

2 pounds Hickory Smoked Tomatoes, page 182

2 whole Hickory Smoked Jalapeños, page 184

¼ medium red onion, peeled and finely chopped

½ cup fresh cilantro sprigs, chopped

1 teaspoon Roasted Garlic Purée, page 88

3 tablespoons extra virgin cold pressed olive oil

1½ tablespoons fresh lime juice

sea salt, to taste

black pepper, freshly ground, to taste

Clancy's Fancy Hot Sauce, or similar, to taste

Roasted Garlic Purée

Makes about 1 cup

1 pound fresh hardnecked garlic, whole heads or similar

½ cup extra virgin cold pressed olive oil

sea salt, to taste

black pepper, freshly ground, to taste

fresh rosemary sprigs

TO ROAST THE GARLIC
Preheat the oven to 375 degrees F.

Peel the outermost layers of skin off the heads of garlic leaving an intact whole head free of any scrap. Split the heads in half cutting across the equator opening the cloves. Put the heads, cut sides up, in a small baking dish and pour the olive oil over them. Season with salt, pepper, and top with the rosemary.

Cover tightly with foil or lid, place in the oven, and roast until about three-fourths cooked, about 45 minutes. Uncover and return to the oven until the cloves begin to pop out of their skins and brown, about 15 minutes.

TO MAKE A PURÉE
When cool enough to handle easily, squeeze the roasted garlic into a small bowl. Press firmly against the skins to extract as much of the sweet roasted garlic as you can.

Add the oil from the baking dish and purée with the back of a spoon or in a small food processor until a paste forms.

Store, tightly covered, in the refrigerator, for up to 1 week.

When choosing garlic, look for well-formed heads with cloves that have grown tightly together. Avoid sprouted garlic or heads that have dark "bruises" or soft spots; these must be removed or they will affect the taste of the entire head.

Although I prefer "hardnecked" garlic (where the center of the garlic heads contain the hard garlic stalk), it's generally not seen in commercial groceries because of the short shelf life. For my taste the "hardneck" varieties have a wider variety and wealth of flavor compared to their "softnecked" cousins, but this recipe works with both varieties.

If you're interested in "hardnecked" varieties of garlic your best bet would be to frequent your local farmers markets and request them.

Can be used as an appetizer with artisan bread and sweet butter or as a garnish for roasted poultry and meats.

The extra olive oil can be strained and used as intensely flavored oil for sautés and vinaigrettes.

Chicken Sugar Beet Skewers with Maple Smoked Jalapeño and Lime Glaze

Peel the sugar beet and cut in half lengthwise. Cut each half into ¼-inch thick slices (like long French fries).

Cut a sharp notch at the end of the beet skewer to allow the skewer to penetrate the chicken.

Thread 2 or 3 pieces of chicken onto a single sugar beet skewer. Repeat the process with the rest of skewers and chicken. Place the skewers in a shallow bowl.

In a small bowl, combine the oil and garlic, salt and pepper; mix well, and then pour the mixture over the chicken skewers. Let marinate, covered and refrigerated, for at least 2 hours.

Preheat a grill or the broiler.

Grill or roast the chicken skewers until they are firm to the touch and cooked through, about 3 minutes per side.

Place the chicken skewers on a serving platter and drizzle with the Maple Smoked Jalapeño and Lime Glaze.

Serves 4–6

1 whole young sugar beet

1 pound chicken tenderloins, or breast cut into ½-inch thick chunks, preferably from Michigan

2 tablespoons extra virgin cold pressed olive oil

1 teaspoon freshly chopped hardnecked garlic

sea salt, to taste

black pepper, freshly ground, to taste

Maple Smoked Jalapeño and Lime Glaze, page 174

Serves 6–8

FOR COOKING SHRIMP

1 quart water, well salted

2 tablespoons fresh lime juice

1 pound fresh white shrimp, preferably from Michigan, or similar, peeled and deveined

FOR COOLING THE SHRIMP

1 quart water, well salted and iced

2 tablespoons fresh lime juice

FOR THE DRESSING

1 large beefsteak tomato, smoked, peeled and seeded

2 large jalapeños, smoked, seeded and chopped

1 large red bell pepper, roasted, peeled and chopped

½ red onion, roasted, peeled and chopped

2 tablespoons Roasted Garlic Purée, page 88

¾ cup fresh lime juice

½ cup fresh apple cider, preferably from Michigan and preferably unpasturized

1 tablespoon maple sugar, preferably from Michigan

Clancy's Fancy Hot Sauce, or similar, to taste

sea salt, to taste

FOR THE GARNISH

1 small red onion, peeled and diced

1 small Honeycrisp apple, preferably from Michigan, or similar, diced

2 tablespoons fresh chives, chopped

2 tablespoons fresh scallions, chopped

¼ cup fresh cilantro, chopped

Great Lakes White Shrimp Ceviche with Smoked Tomatoes and Honeycrisp Apples

Bring 1 quart of nicely salted water (tastes like the sea) to a boil and add 2 table-spoons of the lime juice.

Add the shrimp for approximately 1 to 2 minutes (no longer) then remove to a nicely salted ice bath seasoned with 2 tablespoons of lime juice until cold.

Place the dressing ingredients in the blender and purée. Pour the puréed dressing over the cold shrimp. Mix and chill.

Combine all garnish ingredients and toss with shrimp ceviche before serving.

Recommended beverage: Mawby Cremant Brut

Ceviche is best made the day it is served. Flavorings can be added to the shrimp a few hours in advance.

Legend has it that Latin-American fishermen so savored their catches that they would squeeze fresh Mexican limes over fish caught in the morning and feast on the flavors by lunch. Basically a seafood salad, ceviche, seviche or cebiche is prepared by cutting fresh pieces of fish and "cooking" them in a marinade of that tart Mexican lime with robust and fiery spices. This Latin classic dish never sees the flame of my wood burning oven or the intense heat of my grill; it's the citrus juices that do all the cooking!

Grilled Ears of Michigan Sweet Corn with Black Truffles

Pull all the husks back from each cob of corn without removing it. Pull off and remove all the silk, using a soft brush to get the last strands.

Using a rubber spatula smear 2 tablespoons of softened Black Truffle Compound Butter over each cob of corn. Return the husks to their original position and twist the top. Repeat with all cobs. Refrigerate the corncobs to firm up the butter.

While the butter is firming up, prepare a charcoal or wood fire and let it burn until the coals are medium hot. Set the grill rack 4 inches from the hot coals. Lay the corn on the grill rack and roast for 15 to 20 minutes, turning frequently with tongs. Pull back some husks to test the kernels for doneness. When done, remove from grill, let cool for a few minutes and pull the husks back over the base and trim leaving the stalk to use as a handle for picking up the corn.

Place corn on a serving platter and garnish with Parmesan cheese and a drizzle of white truffle oil. Serve immediately.

Serves 6

6 ears double sweet corn, ultra fresh, preferably from Michigan, in the husk with the stalk stub

12 tablespoons Compound Butter, softened, page 178, add black truffles per recipe instructions

6 teaspoons white truffle oil

⅓ cup Wisantigo Parmesan, or similar, grated

The Maize Craze

Field and sweet corn are big producers for Michigan and the golden fields dot the middle of the mitt. I can't think of anything that screams summer louder than ears of steaming hot sweet corn dripping with local melted butter. Here is a little factoid that I found surprising. In 2002 Michigan cultivated about 2.02 million acres of maize yet only 10,000 acres of sweet corn were harvested for fresh consumption, almost all was harvested for livestock, biodegradable products, and most recently, Ethanol.

Michigan Beer Bread

Makes 1 loaf

3 cups unbleached all-purpose flour, preferably from Michigan

1 tablespoon baking powder

4 tablespoons maple sugar, preferably from Michigan

2 teaspoons sea salt

1 12-ounce artisan beer, preferably from Michigan, at room temperature

2 ounces unsalted butter, melted

coarse sea salt, for garnish

Preheat the oven to 375 degrees F.

In a mixing bowl, combine all the dry ingredients. Add the beer all at once, mixing as little as possible using a rubber spatula. The batter should be lumpy.

Pour the batter into an 8-inch well-seasoned cast iron skillet that has been brushed with some of the melted butter and sprinkle the top with the coarse sea salt or pour the batter into a 9 x 5 x 3-inch bread loaf pan and brush with the melted butter and sprinkle the top with the coarse sea salt.

Bake in the oven for 35 to 40 minutes, or until an inserted skewer comes out clean. Turn out onto a rack to cool.

Michigan Double Sweet Corn Chowder

Serves 4

4 tablespoons unsalted sweet butter

1 cup white onions, peeled and diced

½ cup leeks, white part only, diced

1 tablespoon Roasted Garlic Purée, page 88

½ pound red skin potatoes, washed and sliced

9–10 ears ultra fresh double sweet corn, preferably from Michigan, shucked, kernels removed, reserving "bones"(ears)

3½–4 cups heavy cream

sea salt, to taste

Clancy's Fancy Hot Sauce, or similar, to taste

½ small lemon, juiced

In a 3-quart saucepan, melt the butter; sauté the onions and leeks over a moderate heat until translucent and wilted, about 10 minutes.

Add the Roasted Garlic Purée and the sliced red skin potatoes. Cook another 3 minutes or until the potatoes are warmed and completely coated in the butter. Add the heavy cream, "corn bones" and season with the salt and hot sauce.

Simmer for 20 to 30 minutes or until the potatoes are tender and the "bones" have released their flavor, remove and discard the "bones."

Place the rest of the raw corn kernels in the bottom of a soup tureen and pour the hot soup base over all, season to taste with the lemon juice.

Serve immediately.

Recommended beverage: Shady Lane Chardonnay

White Shrimp with Garlic

In a medium cast iron skillet, heat olive oil over a medium heat. When the oil is hot add the garlic. Sizzle until golden in color, stirring all the time, about 1 to 2 minutes. Add the chiles and leave for 1 minute.

Turn off the heat just as the garlic starts to turn brown. (If the garlic turns brown you have overcooked it and will need to start again.)

Add the whole shrimp and sauté quickly, stirring all the time for about 2 minutes or until the shrimp are cooked. Season to taste with the Maple Salt.

Serve in the hot cast iron skillet with plenty of fresh artisan bread for soaking up the rich flavorful oil.

Recommended beverage: Peninsula Cellars Pinot Blanc

Serves 4–6

1 cup extra virgin cold pressed olive oil

3 large cloves fresh hardnecked garlic, peeled and thinly sliced

1 large dried aji amarillo chile pepper, broken

2 pounds white shrimp, preferably from Michigan, or similar, head and shells intact

Maple Salt, to taste, page 178

1 lemon, cut into eights

artisan bread

unkle e's ramblings on shrimp!

A shrimp is a shrimp; and a prawn is, well, a shrimp. Whoever wrote the lyrics, "you say tomato, I say toe-mah-toe" could just as well have added the verse, "you say shrimp, I say prawn." These two words are used interchangeably in markets and restaurants everywhere. Textbooks may agree that a shrimp is a shrimp, but many people and quite a few cookbooks and chefs refer to this country's most popular shellfish as a prawn. Some say the difference is size. In many parts of our country, small and medium shrimp are sold simply as shrimp, while large, extra-large and jumbo shrimp are called prawns. Unfortunately, this "rule" doesn't always hold. In some areas, all shrimp, small and large, are sold as shrimp, while in other regions; all you'll find are prawns. Purists (including yours truly) may argue that the term "prawn" is reserved for the shrimp's close relative, the Dublin bay prawn. The Dublin bay prawn resembles a shrimp, but it's distinguished by its small pincer claws (similar to those on a lobster) and a narrower body. Sometimes called Florida or Caribbean lobsterettes or French langoustines, alas these shellfish are almost unavailable in your local markets.

For many people shrimp is the premier seafood and demand for the curvy crustaceans is at an all-time high. But shrimp fishing and production can be highly destructive to the environment. For example, ten pounds of other sea creatures are usually just thrown away as by-catch, when just one pound of wild shrimp is taken from the oceans. As you can imagine that practice has decimated fish populations in shrimping waters. In recent years, people in tropical regions have taken to shrimp farming, but at the expense of mangrove swamps. These shrimp farms often have to be closed within a few years, after waste problems lead to all sorts of ookey infections. But all is not lost my Great Lakes gastronauts. The magical mitten's first shrimp farmer says he has an answer: grow the salt-water shrimp indoors! Yessiree, our old pal Russ Allen bought his six acres in Okemos to do something that's never been done successfully before—to mass-produce salt-water shrimp indoors.

Popcorn Shrimp

Combine the rice flour, with one teaspoon each of the sea salt and black pepper in a large zip-top plastic bag.

Place the beaten egg whites in a shallow dish seasoned with 1 teaspoon each of the salt and pepper.

Place the popcorn flour in a shallow dish seasoned with the remaining salt and pepper.

Place the cleaned shrimp in bag with rice flour, salt and pepper; shake to coat well.

Carefully dip each shrimp in the egg white mixture, and roll in Popcorn Flour mixture.

Fry shrimp, in batches, in 2 inches hot oil (375 degrees F) until golden.

Serve immediately.

Serves 4

⅓ cup rice flour

3 teaspoons sea salt, or to taste

3 teaspoons black pepper, freshly ground, or to taste

3 egg whites, beaten lightly

1 cup Popcorn Flour, recipe below

1½ pounds white shrimp, preferably from Michigan, or similar, peeled and deveined

soybean oil, preferably from Michigan, for deep-frying

Popcorn Flour

TO COOK THE POPCORN

Place 2 tablespoons of the Michigan soybean oil and scatter a few unpopped corn kernels in a 3 to 4 quart heavy bottomed stockpot; cover and heat over medium-high heat until the first kernel pops. Add the rest of corn kernels to the pot and cover.

When you hear the kernels start popping, shake the pot frequently to keep popcorn from burning. When the sound of the popping stops, immediately remove the pan from the heat and pour the hot popcorn on a cookie sheet to cool.

TO GRIND THE POPCORN

Working in small batches, place the cooled and popped corn into a blender or coffee mill and process or grind until the popcorn resembles a very coarse meal similar to cornmeal.

Store unused flour in airtight container in the freezer.

Makes about 4 cups

½ cup popcorn kernels, preferably from Michigan

2 tablespoons soybean oil, preferably from Michigan

½ cup unpopped popcorn will make about 8 cups of popped corn. This will yield about 4 cups of flour.

Pop corn in hot air popper or use another method that does not use oil. Discard unpopped kernels.

Sweet Potato Taco with Hickory Smoked Tomato Cream

Serves 4

FOR THE TACOS

2 medium sweet potatoes

4 large flour tortillas

1 cup white cheddar cheese, grated

¼ cup Wisantigo Parmesan, or similar, grated

½ cup fresh cilantro, chopped

sea salt, to taste

black pepper, freshly ground, to taste

½ cup clover honey, preferably from Michigan

2 tablespoons extra virgin cold pressed olive oil

FOR THE HICKORY SMOKED TOMATO CREAM

1½ cups Hickory Smoked Tomato Salsa, page 87

1 cup heavy cream

4 cilantro sprigs

Preheat the oven to 400 degrees F.

Place potatoes on large baking sheet, bake until soft, 35 to 40 minutes for medium potatoes, up to 1 hour for large. Let the potatoes cool, then peel and coarsely mash, reserve.

Using 1 tortilla for each serving, place a quarter of each cheese over the top half of the tortilla's surface, top with a quarter of the mashed sweet potatoes and the cilantro. Season with salt and pepper to taste.

Roll tortilla over the filling to make a cigar. Before serving brush the top lightly with oil. Bake for 8–10 minutes or until the filling is warm and the tortillas are crisp.

While the tacos are heating place a medium non-reactive saucepan over medium-high heat with the Hickory Smoked Tomato Salsa and the heavy cream. Bring to a boil and reduce heat a bit to reduce the sauce for 3 to 5 minutes or until the sauce is thick and creamy.

Divide the sauce between four dinner plates and top with the hot taco cut on a bias. Drizzle each with the remaining clover honey, a bit of the Parmesan, and garnish with the cilantro sprigs.

Recommended beverage: Chateau Grand Traverse Gamay Noir Reserve

Wood Roasted Pumpkin Risotto

Serves 6

1 medium pie pumpkin, for serving

2½ cups pumpkin flesh, cut (½-inch), peeled, seeded (save the seeds)

sea salt, to taste

black pepper, freshly ground, to taste

1 teaspoon Saigon cinnamon, ground

½ teaspoon ginger, ground

½ teaspoon nutmeg, ground

3–4 tablespoons maple sugar, preferably from Michigan

extra virgin cold pressed olive oil, to taste

6–8 cups vegetable broth

2 tablespoons extra virgin cold pressed olive oil

1 small red onion, peeled and finely chopped

sea salt, to taste

black pepper, freshly ground, to taste

Clancy's Fancy Hot Sauce, or similar, to taste

2 cups carnaroli or Arborio short grain white rice

1 cup dry white wine, preferably from Michigan

½ cup Roasted Garlic Purée, page 88

2 tablespoons fresh thyme, chopped

2 ounces Wisantigo Parmesan, or similar, grated

2 tablespoons unsalted sweet butter

Preheat oven to 350 degrees F.

Carefully cut out the top of the pumpkin (being careful not to break it). Scoop out seeds and reserve. Roast the whole pumpkin and the top in a medium roasting pan with ½-inch water. Cover tightly with foil and bake until very tender, 45 to 50 minutes. Cool slightly. Discard water from roasting pan, then return pumpkin shell to the pan and keep warm, covered with foil.

Place the raw diced pumpkin in a suitable roasting pan and season with salt, pepper, cinnamon, ginger, nutmeg and maple sugar. Toss well with the olive oil and roast the pumpkin until tender, 10 to 15 minutes. Let the mixture cool to room temperature and blend to a fine purée in a food processor, reserve.

While the whole pumpkin and diced pumpkin roasts prepare the risotto.

In a large, heavy bottomed stockpot over high heat bring vegetable broth to a boil; reduce heat and cover, keeping it ready at stove-side.

In a large heavy bottomed non-reactive sauté pan, heat the olive oil over low heat and "sweat" the red onions until translucent about 3 to 5 minutes. Begin light seasoning with the salt, pepper and hot sauce.

Increase the heat to medium-high and add the rice, continue the sauté until the rice is well coated with the oil and the grains are slightly toasted, stirring with a wooden spoon, about 5 to 8 minutes. (A wooden spoon is always preferable when making risotto, as a metal spoon tends to cut or injure the grains of rice.)

Once the rice is toasted, add the white wine.

After the rice has absorbed the white wine and the skillet is nearly dry, begin adding the hot vegetable broth one cup at a time, stirring constantly and letting each addition be absorbed before adding the next, until the rice is tender and creamy looking but still al dente, about 18 to 20 minutes total. (There may be broth left over.) Adding the liquid in stages, instead of all at once, allows the grains of rice to expand more fully, adding to the risotto's creamy texture.

Halfway through the cooking process add the Roasted Garlic Purée and continue with the light seasoning of salt, pepper and hot sauce to taste.

Remove the pan from heat and stir in the roasted pumpkin purée, cheese, fresh thyme and butter, stirring until butter and cheese have melted. Taste and season if necessary, with salt, pepper, and hot sauce.

Place the roasted pumpkin shell on a suitable platter, fill with the hot risotto, and cover with the reserved top. Serve immediately.

Great Lakes White Shrimp Stuffing

Preheat oven to 325 degrees F.

In a large heavy bottomed skillet over medium heat melt the butter. Add the fennel, carrot, celery, leek and onion, sea salt and black pepper. Stew over medium-high heat, stirring frequently, until vegetables are lightly caramelized, about 10 to 15 minutes. Remove from the heat, let cool to room temperature and reserve.

In a large mixing bowl, whisk eggs, Roasted Garlic Purée and 2 cups Shrimp Stock (or the optional combination of Shrimp Stock and heavy cream) together. Add bread and stir until coated evenly. Add the raw shrimp, the cooked vegetables with all the butter, thyme, chives and lemon juice. If bread cubes seem dry, add additional Shrimp Stock/heavy cream. Add salt and pepper to taste.

In a suitable shallow baking dish bake the stuffing for 30 minutes (for moist stuffing, bake covered entire time; for less moist stuffing with a slightly crisp top, uncover halfway through baking time).

Serve immediately.

> We found that a combination of equal parts shrimp stock and heavy cream made this dish even more luxurious. But feel free to use whatever your waistlines and wallets require. If shrimp stock is unavailable equal amounts of clam juice, vegetable broth or light poultry stock may be used in its place.

Serves 10–12

1½ pounds unsalted sweet butter

2 cups whole fennel bulbs, trimmed and diced

1 cup whole carrots, peeled and diced

1 cup large celery stalks, diced

1 cup large leeks, washed and diced

1 cup large red onion, peeled and diced

sea salt, to taste

black pepper, freshly ground, to taste

6 large eggs, lightly beaten

½ cup Roasted Garlic Purée, page 88

4–8 cups Shrimp Stock, page 173, or a combination of equal parts of Shrimp Stock and heavy cream

2 pounds day old artisan bread, crusts trimmed and cubed

3 pounds white shrimp, preferably from Michigan, or similar, peeled, deveined and butterflied

3 tablespoons fresh thyme, chopped

3 tablespoons fresh chives, chopped

½ cup lemon juice, freshly squeezed

Shrimp Stuffed Mushrooms

Preheat the oven to 350 degrees F.

Place mushroom caps on a baking sheet lined with parchment paper or an oiled heat-proof casserole.

Place a heaping tablespoon of the shrimp stuffing mixture into the cap of each mushroom and top with the grated Parmesan.

Bake the mushroom caps for 30 minutes.

Serve immediately.

Makes 16–20

16–20 large white mushrooms, cleaned and stems removed

1 pound Great Lakes White Shrimp Stuffing, recipe above

2 ounces Wisantigo Parmesan, or similar, grated

Carrot Couscous with White Shrimp and Chives

In a large, heavy bottomed non-reactive saucepan bring first 4 ingredients to a simmer over medium-high heat. Add the shrimp and cook for a few minutes or until the shrimp are slightly underdone (they will continue to cook with the couscous).

Meanwhile place the couscous in a large heatproof bowl. Pour the carrot mixture and the slightly underdone shrimp over the couscous and gently stir to combine. Cover the bowl tightly with plastic wrap and let stand 5 to 10 minutes or until the couscous has absorbed all the carrot mixture and the shrimp is plump. Remove the plastic wrap and discard. Drizzle with oil, and fluff with a fork. Sprinkle with chives and toss to combine.

Serves 2

⅔ cup carrot juice, freshly juiced (one pound of carrots will make approximately six to eight ounces of carrot juice)

1½ teaspoons lemon juice, freshly juiced

¼ teaspoon sea salt

⅛ teaspoon black pepper, freshly ground, or to taste

8 ounces white shrimp, preferably from Michigan, or similar, peeled, deveined and butterflied

½ cup couscous, plain

2 teaspoons extra virgin cold pressed olive oil

2 tablespoons chives, freshly chopped

Fried Chicken and Buttermilk Waffles with Thyme Lime Honey

Serves 6–8

Basic Maple Brine, page 108

one 3–5 pound fryer chicken, brined and cut up into 8 or 10 pieces*

1 whole red onion, peeled and sliced into rounds

FOR THE CHICKEN COATING

3 cups rice flour

2½ tablespoons dried thyme

2½ tablespoons sea salt

1½ tablespoons sweet paprika

1½ tablespoons aji amarillo powder

FOR THE BUTTERMILK MARINADE

2¼ cups cultured buttermilk

½ cup Roasted Garlic Purée, page 88

2 tablespoons sea salt

1 tablespoon Clancy's Fancy Hot Sauce, or similar

2 quarts lard or peanut oil, for frying

10 large sprigs fresh thyme, for flavoring the lard and garnish

10 cloves fresh hardnecked garlic, peeled for flavoring the lard and garnish

sea salt, to taste

black pepper, freshly ground, to taste

1 whole lime, cut into 8ths for garnish

Buttermilk Cornmeal Waffles, page 110

Thyme Lime Honey, page 180

Prepare the brine and brine the whole bird 12 to 24 hours. After brining, drain the bird and discard the brine.

In a large mixing bowl combine the buttermilk, Roasted Garlic Purée, salt, and hot sauce and blend well. Add the brined chicken pieces and marinate at least 1 hour and up to 4.

Place the red onion rings in a bowl of ice water and reserve.

Place the rice flour, dried thyme, salt, paprika and aji amarillo powder in a large brown paper grocery bag and mix well. Remove the chicken pieces from the buttermilk (reserve buttermilk for the onions) and drop into the paper bag 2 or 3 at a time and shake to coat. At this point you may want to "double dip" meaning dip the coated chicken pieces back in the buttermilk and back in the flour for a heavier coating. Place the coated pieces of chicken on a wire rack, set aside to rest while you prepare the lard.

In a 5-quart cast iron skillet (or similar), add about 2 quarts of lard. It should not come up more than halfway the height of the pan for safety.

Add the thyme sprigs and garlic cloves to the cool lard and heat over medium-high heat until the oil registers 350 degrees F on a deep-fry thermometer.

Once the lard has reached 350 degrees F, working in batches, carefully add the chicken pieces 3 or 4 at a time.

As the thyme and garlic crisp, remove from the lard and drain on paper towels and reserve for garnish.

Fry the chicken, turning the pieces once, until golden brown and cooked through, about 8 to 12 minutes. Total cooking time should be about 30 minutes. Repeat with the remaining chicken pieces.

Reserve the cooked chicken on a wire cooling rack over a cookie sheet in a warm oven. Season to taste with a bit of sea salt and cracked black pepper.

After all the chicken is cooked, drain and dry the onions rings and repeat the same procedure as the chicken by dropping them in the reserved buttermilk and then into the rice flour.

Fry the onion rings in the lard at the same temperature until crisp, about 35 minutes, drain on paper towels, season and reserve.

While the onions are cooking prepare the Buttermilk Cornmeal Waffles (page 110) and reserve in a warm oven.

On a large serving platter scatter the waffles and top with the fried chicken pieces. Garnish with the onion rings, crisped thyme sprigs and garlic and lime wedges. Serve the Thyme Lime Honey on the side.

Recommended Beverage: Bel Lago Chardonnay

CUTTING UP THE CHICKEN
*Remove the backbone from the bird (save for broth or discard or season and fry with the chicken parts) and remove the two chicken wings and fold akimbo. Remove the leg/thigh pieces and cut in two for two legs and two thighs. If the chicken is on the smaller size leave the breasts whole for 8 pieces total. If the chicken is on the heavier side of 5 pounds cut the breasts in two for ten pieces total. The idea is to have all the pieces of chicken approximately the same size for even cooking.

Feel free to substitute any fresh seasonal herb to compliment the chicken garnish and coordinate it with the dried herb in the chicken coating.

Buttermilk Cornmeal Waffles

Makes 2 large Belgian-style waffles

1 cup unbleached all-purpose flour, preferably from Michigan

1 cup cornmeal, preferably from Michigan, coarse grind, yellow or white

½ teaspoon baking soda

2 teaspoons baking powder

1 teaspoon sea salt

2 large whole eggs, beaten

4 tablespoons unsalted sweet butter, melted and slightly cooled

1¾ cups cultured buttermilk

Preheat waffle iron according to manufacturer's directions.

In a medium bowl whisk together the flour, cornmeal, baking soda, baking powder, and salt. In another bowl beat together eggs with the slightly cooled melted butter, and then add the buttermilk.

Add the wet ingredients to the dry and stir until combined. Allow to rest for at least 5 minutes.

Ladle the recommended amount of waffle batter onto the iron and cook the waffles according to the manufacturer's recommendations.

Serve immediately or keep warm in a 200 degree F oven until ready to serve.

Corn flour offers a finer, smoother waffle and can be substituted for the cornmeal. Also, the eggs may be separated with the whites being beaten until stiff, then gently folded into the batter for a lighter waffle.

Minted White Chocolate Truffles

Combine the white chocolate and butter in a heatproof mixing bowl. Place the bowl over a pan of hot but not simmering water to melt, stirring constantly.

Remove the bowl from the water and slowly add the cold cream and the peppermint oil a bit at a time until smooth.

In the bowl of a mixer fitted with the paddle attachment beat the white chocolate at medium speed until it gets thick and light colored, about 4 to 5 minutes. Spread over the bottom of a baking dish and smooth the top.

Refrigerate about 2 hours, or until firm.

Place the powdered sugar in a deep plate or shallow bowl. Use a melon baller or tablespoon to scoop out balls of white chocolate about the size of a walnut; set them on the plate with the powdered sugar and roll using 2 forks to completely coat with the sugar. Then use the forks to carefully transfer them to a parchment lined baking sheet.

Can be refrigerated up to 2 weeks.

Recommended beverage: M. Lawrence Fizz Sparkling

Makes about 1 dozen

12 ounces white chocolate, high quality

4 tablespoons unsalted sweet butter

6 tablespoons heavy cream, chilled

8–10 drops peppermint oil, preferably from Michigan

1 cup powdered sugar, for dusting

Paczki, (pronounced POONCH-key) is basically a deep-fried jelly filled donut traditionally stuffed with fillings like rosebud, raspberry, or prune marmalades or the more common vanilla cream. The best are said to come from the Polish Bakeries in Hamtramck that crank them out in amazing numbers in the days leading up to "Fat Tuesday" after which the Polish Christians swear off confections for the 40 days of lent.

Turkey Cranberry Sausages

Makes about 12, 4-ounce sausages

2½ pounds well-chilled turkey thigh meat, skin attached and boned

¾ pound well-chilled Maple Cured Hickory Smoked Bacon, or similar, page 153

¾ pound dried cranberries

1 tablespoon sea salt

2 teaspoons black pepper, freshly ground, or to taste

1 tablespoon thyme, dried

1 tablespoon sage, dried

1 tablespoon paprika

2 teaspoons maple syrup, preferably from Michigan

¼ cup Roasted Garlic Purée, page 88

½ cup poultry stock, vegetable stock or water

½ cup hard apple cider, or sweet, preferably from Michigan

hog casings, rinsed

Set up your meat grinder according to the manufacturer's directions.

In a large mixing bowl add the turkey meat and the bacon. Toss with the cranberries, salt, pepper, thyme, sage and paprika. Put the seasoned turkey meats and cranberries through the ¼-inch or small plate of a sausage grinder. Add the maple syrup, Roasted Garlic Purée, stock and cider to the ground meat and mix thoroughly with your hands.

According to your grinders directions stuff the mix into the hog casings and tie off at 4 to 6 inch lengths. Poach the sausages in salted water for about 10 to 15 minutes or until cooked through. Let cool in the poaching water and refrigerate.

Recommended beverage: Fenn Valley Semi-Dry Riesling

Mashed Sweet Potatoes with Horseradish

Serves 6–8

3 pounds large sweet potatoes

¼ cup unsalted sweet butter

1 teaspoon sea salt

2 tablespoons maple syrup, preferably from Michigan

2 tablespoons horseradish, prepared in vinegar, drained

Preheat the oven to 400 degrees F.

Place sweet potatoes on a baking sheet and roast until easily pierced with a fork, about 1 hour.

Peel the sweet potatoes while still hot. Combine the potatoes, butter, salt, maple syrup, and horseradish in a large bowl.

Mash with a potato masher until the potatoes are smooth. Serve immediately.

Poached Breast of Chicken with Fresh Carrot and Ginger Sauce

In a medium saucepan combine the chicken breasts with enough cold water to cover them by 1-inch. Remove the chicken, bring the water to a boil, and add salt to taste. Return the chicken to the pan and poach it at a bare simmer for 17 minutes. Remove the pan from the heat. Let the chicken cool in the liquid for 30 minutes and drain it.

While the breasts are poaching prepare the Fresh Carrot and Ginger Sauce.

Plate the chicken breasts and strain the hot sauce over the top.

Serve immediately.

Recommended beverage: Shady Lane Chardonnay

Serves 2

two 8-ounce breasts of chicken, boneless, with the skin, preferably from Michigan

Fresh Carrot and Ginger Sauce, recipe below

Fresh Carrot Sauce with Ginger

In a small non-reactive sauce pot over medium-high heat place the carrot juice, ginger, lime juice, hot sauce and salt. Reduce by half until juice starts to thicken. Add the cold butter and shake the pan to incorporate the butter and emulsify the sauce. Taste and adjust seasonings as necessary. Use immediately.

Makes about ½ cup

1 cup fresh carrot juice

one 1-inch long piece of ginger, peeled and bruised

1 tablespoon fresh lime juice

1 shot Clancy's Fancy Hot Sauce, or similar

sea salt, to taste

1 tablespoon unsalted sweet butter, cold

Juicing fresh carrots with a juicer is best. Now many grocery stores are selling fresh carrot juice.

One pound of carrots will make approximately six to eight ounces of carrot juice.

Potato and Cheese Ravioli Topped With Mixed Vegetable Vinaigrette

Wash and peel the potatoes. Put them into well salted, boiling water until the potatoes are just tender (it is very important not to under or overcook them). Drain them and let them sit for about 5 minutes to enable the excess water to evaporate (if you overcook them or don't drain them correctly they'll be too moist and your filling will be too wet).

When the potatoes have cooled slightly add your butter, Roasted Garlic Purée and the grated cheeses. Stir and mash with a fork or potato masher to mix and break the potatoes up.

Add the nutmeg and seasoning to taste and stir in the herbs. Stuff the ravioli using the fresh wonton wrappers with a good heaping teaspoon of this mixture. Seal edges with a bit of water and crimp with a fork. Cook in boiling salted water for about 3 to 4 minutes, until tender.

Serve the hot raviolis topped with the Mixed Vegetable Vinaigrette, grated Parmesan and reserved mixed herbs over the top.

Recommended beverage: Peninsula Cellars Gewurztraminer Manigold

Serves 4

1¼ pounds all-purpose potatoes, preferably from Michigan

¼ cup unsalted sweet butter

1 tablespoon Roasted Garlic Purée, page 88

4 ounces white cheddar, grated, preferably from Michigan

2 ounces Wisantigo Parmesan, or similar, grated

nutmeg, freshly grated

sea salt, to taste

black pepper, freshly ground, to taste

2 tablespoons mixed fresh herbs, large stalks removed, plus extra for garnish

1 pound wonton wrappers, fresh

Mixed Vegetable Vinaigrette, page 116

Posen, Michigan has hosted the Potato Festival for the past 55 years for the simple reason that Michigan does the spud proud. It's the cool moist climate and deep sandy/loamy soil that make Michigan the nations leading producer of new red skin potatoes and "chippers" for Americans number one treat — 'tater chips!

Mixed Vegetable Vinaigrette

Serves 4

1½ pounds cherry tomatoes, preferably from Michigan, stemmed and cut
in half stem to core

¾ pounds haricots verts (thin French
green beans), trimmed

1 pound "baby" Patty pan squash,
trimmed

4 bunches of baby carrots (about 24),
trimmed and peeled if necessary

3 bunches of small radishes (about
24), trimmed and cut in half stem
to core

FOR THE VINAIGRETTE

1 large shallot, peeled and chopped

1 tablespoon Roasted Garlic Purée,
page 88

2 teaspoons coarse grained mustard

4 tablespoons lime juice, freshly
squeezed

⅓ cup extra virgin cold pressed
olive oil

In a saucepan of boiling salted water cook separately the haricots verts, squash, and carrots for 3 to 5 minutes each, or until each vegetable is crisp-tender, transferring them as they are cooked with a slotted spoon to a bowl of ice and cold salted water to stop the cooking. Transfer the vegetables with the slotted spoon to paper towels and pat them dry.

In the saucepan of boiling salted water cook the radishes for 2 to 3 minutes, or until they are crisp-tender, and transfer them with the slotted spoon to the bowl of ice and salted cold water. Drain the radishes and pat them dry. Transfer the vegetables to the refrigerator and chill them covered. The vegetables may be cooked 6 days in advance and kept covered and refrigerated.

FOR THE VINAIGRETTE

In a bar blender or food processor blend together the shallots, Roasted Garlic Purée, mustard, lime juice, and salt and pepper to taste until the mixture is smooth. With the machine running add the oil in a stream, and blend the dressing until it is emulsified.

When ready to serve combine all the vegetables and the cherry tomatoes in a large sauté pan over medium high heat and add the vinaigrette. Gently and quickly heat the vegetables coating evenly with the dressing.

Serve with Potato and Cheese Raviolis, page 115.

unkle e's ramblings on blanching!

Blanching vegetables is a very easy but important technique that requires plenty of boiling water and plenty of salt. Don't be scared but for perfectly cooked and seasoned vegetables about one cup of salt for every gallon of water is necessary. Keep in mind that the vegetables will be uniformly and perfectly seasoned at this point and depending on what they will be used for very little if any additional salt will be needed.

During cooking for green vegetables acids and enzymes are released that can dull the beautiful green color. By using large amounts of water the acids and enzymes are diluted (the more water the more dilution) which means the more water the more color we get to keep in our vegetables.

Big Soft Pretzels

Serves 6

3 tablespoons maple sugar, preferably from Michigan

1 (¼ oz) package or (2½ teaspoons) active dry yeast

1 cup water, warmed (105 to 110 degrees F)

1 tablespoon sea salt

5 cups unbleached all-purpose flour, preferably from Michigan

¼ cup baking soda

3½ quarts water, for boiling the pretzels

1 large egg, lightly beaten with a bit of salt, for glazing

coarse pretzel salt or kosher salt, for sprinkling on the pretzels

TO PROOF AND PREPARE THE YEAST

Stir together maple sugar, yeast, and 1 cup lukewarm water (105 to 110 degrees F) in a glass measuring cup or small bowl, then let stand until foamy, about 5 minutes. (If mixture doesn't foam or "proof", you need to discard and begin again with new yeast.)

TO MAKE THE DOUGH

Add the 5 cups of unbleached flour and 1 tablespoon of sea salt in bowl of a stand mixer. Add the proofed yeast mixture and blend slowly with the dough hook until the dough masses together. Gradually increase the speed to medium adding additional flour if necessary to achieve a smooth sticky dough (the dough should retain a sheen and not appear too floury). Allow to run about 6 to 8 minutes.

Remove the bowl from the machine and cover tightly with plastic wrap, then let dough rise in a draft-free place (an empty off oven is perfect) at room temperature until doubled in bulk, about 45 minutes.

TO SHAPE THE PRETZELS

Turn out dough onto a clean work surface and into 6 equal strips and roll each out like a rope. Using your palms, roll 1 piece back and forth on a clean dry work surface into a horseshoe shape with the bottom of the horseshoe closest to you. Pull the ends towards each other as if you were making a circle but instead cross, then wrap one around each other placing each end on opposite sides of the pretzel loop. If dough sticks to your hands, lightly dust them with additional flour.

Transfer pretzel with your hands to an oiled baking sheet and repeat with the rest of the dough in same manner, spacing them 1½ inches apart. Let pretzels stand, uncovered, about 20 minutes. Meanwhile, put oven rack in upper third of oven and preheat oven to 425 degrees F.

TO BOIL THE PRETZELS

Bring a wide 6-quart pot filled with 3½ quarts of water to a boil with the baking soda.

Using both hands, carefully add the pretzels 1, 2 or 3 at a time (depending on the circumference of your pot), to the boiling water and cook for about 2 minutes, turning over once with tongs, until pretzels are puffed and shape is set, about a minute or about 3 minutes total. Transfer parboiled pretzels to a rack to cool. Repeat with the remaining pretzels in batches if necessary.

TO BAKE THE PRETZELS

Line baking sheet with parchment paper, oil, then arrange pretzels on sheet. Brush pretzels lightly with some of egg and sprinkle with pretzel salt. Bake until golden brown and lightly crusted, about 20 to 30 minutes.

Cool 15 minutes, then serve warm with ballpark mustard.

Spicy Chicken Wings with Clancy's Fancy Hot Splash

Preheat the oven to 400 degrees F.

Brine the chicken wings for at least 6 hours or overnight. Lightly rinse and pat dry.

In a large, heavy-bottomed pot, pour in the oil to a depth of 2 inches. Place over medium heat and heat until a deep-fry thermometer inserted in the oil registers 375 degrees F. Working in safe small batches (based on the size and manufacturers directions) fry the brined chicken wings until lightly browned, about 10 to 12 minutes per batch. Using a slotted spoon, transfer the wings to a paper towel-lined plate. (Make sure the oil returns to the proper temperature before frying each batch.)

FOR THE CLANCY'S FANCY HOT SPLASH

In a large bowl, combine all the ingredients for the splash. Taste and adjust seasonings to your taste. Toss the hot fried wings in the hot sauce mixture. Transfer the wings, with the sauce to a suitable roasting pan and bake, turning the wings occasionally, until crispy and very tender, and they have absorbed most of the sauce, about 35 minutes.

Transfer the wings to a serving platter and serve with the Maytag Blue Cheese Cream and celery sticks. Drizzle maple syrup over the wings and serve more splash on the side as a dip if needed.

Serves 4–6

5 pounds whole chicken wings, folded akimbo

Basic Maple Brine, page 173

FOR THE CLANCY'S FANCY HOT SPLASH

1½–2 quarts soybean oil, preferably from Michigan, for frying

1 tablespoon Clancy's Fancy Hot Sauce, or similar, for mild

2 tablespoons Clancy's Fancy Hot Sauce, or similar, for hot

3 tablespoons Clancy's Fancy Hot Sauce, or similar, for extra hot

1 cup raw apple cider vinegar, preferably from Michigan

2 tablespoons Dijon mustard

¼ cup maple syrup, preferably from Michigan

1 teaspoon sea salt, or to taste

FOR SERVING

Maytag Blue Cheese Cream, page 176

celery sticks

¼ cup maple syrup

Is there anybody who doesn't like French fries? With trans-fatty acids and a whole host of other ookey problems associated with fried fun, the food police have given anything crispy a bad name. Not to worry my young gastronauts, I have come to your rescue with my herbed frites borrowing the French term 'cause of the care I take in treating these tasty taters.

I cut unpeeled jumbo Idaho russets thin and long and cook 'em twice in pure clean soybean oil, preferably from Michigan, for maximum flavor and texture. Then I shower the golden sticks with mixed dry herbs, sea salt, black pepper and a bit of garlic oil. Damn-these-spuds-rawk!

Idaho Potato "Pommes Frites"

Serves 4

4 large Idaho potatoes

soybean oil for deep-frying, preferably from Michigan

sea salt, to taste

black pepper, freshly ground, to taste

mixed dried herbs, to taste

garlic-herb infused oil, to taste

Cut the washed and unpeeled potatoes lengthwise into slices ⅜-inch thick. Then cut each slice lengthwise into strips ⅜-inch wide, or use a really expensive French fry cutter. Rinse potatoes in three changes of cold water or until the water runs clear. Place in a bowl filled with ice water and let stand for 5 minutes.

Pour the oil to a depth of at least 3 inches into a deep-fat fryer with a basket or into a deep, heavy pan. If using a deep fat fryer load the oil per manufacturers directions. Whenever using a pan for deep frying never fill more than half way with oil to prevent boil-over. Heat to 325 degrees F, checking the temperature on a built-in thermostat or a deep-fat frying thermometer. If you do not have a thermometer, drop in a piece of potato; the oil should immediately begin to foam along its edges.

While the oil is heating, line platters or trays with paper towels. Drain the potatoes or use a salad spinner and thoroughly dry them with kitchen towels. (Wet potatoes may stick together and will cause the oil to splatter.) If using a fryer, briefly immerse the basket in the hot oil to prevent the potatoes from sticking to it once they are added. Remove the basket from the oil, place 2 handfuls of the potatoes in the basket and lower into the oil. Alternatively, carefully lower them in the pan of oil using a skimmer or tongs. The oil will expand and cover the potatoes. Be sure not to add too many potatoes at one time or they will not cook evenly. Fry until the potatoes are just beginning to brown, about 10 minutes. Remove the basket and set it over a bowl to drain, then transfer the frites to paper towel-lined trays or platters for at least 10 minutes or for up to 2 hours. If removing with a skimmer or tongs, place the frites directly on lined trays.

Just before serving, line additional trays or platters with paper towels. Reheat the oil to 375 degrees F and fry the potatoes again in batches until golden brown and crisp, about 2 minutes. Remove the basket and set it over a bowl to drain, then turn the finished frites out onto the lined trays, or remove with a skimmer, draining well over the pan, and transfer to lined trays. Season with the sea salt, pepper, mixed herbs and garlic-herb infused oil. Toss well. It is extremely important that the finished frites are seasoned immediately after draining. When the frites are hot the seasoning actually "sticks" to the potatoes. If left to cool first the fries won't hold the seasonings.

Serve immediately.

If all of that time in front of the fryer is a bit of a hassle for you katz-n-kittenz I have found that the frites can be frozen after the first cooking. This way you can prepare oodles of servings that can be stashed in your freezer and simply pull what you need for a flash fry!

Cream of Grilled Tomato Soup

Preheat a gas or solid fuel grill.

Place the whole tomatoes core side up and grill the tomatoes until completely black turning once—and I do mean, black!

Using kitchen tongs carefully remove tomatoes and place in a heavy bottomed and non-reactive saucepan along with any charred tomato skins that might be sticking to the grill.

Roughly break up the soft tomatoes with a large spoon. Begin seasoning with the salt, pepper and hot sauce to taste and continue the seasoning to taste throughout the duration of the preparation.

Bring the grilled tomatoes to a boil. Reduce the heat to low, and simmer uncovered, stirring frequently and reduce until a very thick purée remains (about 4–5 cups). Remove from heat.

Using an immersion blender process the thick tomato purée in the saucepan until smooth or place the grilled tomato mixture in the bowl of a food processor or blender, and purée soup in batches until smooth (If small seeds or bits of charred skin bother you the purée may be run through a fine strainer at this point).

Return the purée to the pan and stir in the cream until well blended. Check the seasonings. Simmer until heated through, 3 to 5 minutes, taste again and re-season if necessary.

Serve immediately.

Serves 4–6

5 pounds red or yellow beefsteak tomatoes (cores removed)

sea salt, to taste

black pepper, freshly ground, to taste

Clancy's Fancy Hot Sauce, or similar, to taste

2–3 cups heavy cream

—€ How much to reduce the grilled tomato base? Well, that's the question of the day isn't it?! When you're talking about soups and sauces of this nature the farther you reduce the base the more intense the flavor will be and the less soup you will have—but what a soup!

—€ How much cream to add? Well, that's the second question of the day!! The more cream that is added the more you will dilute the soup, which is to say, makes it less tomato-ey. In recipe situations like this it's always preferable to add half of the recipe's recommendation and then proceed to your taste.

—€ So as you can see this "recipe" is more of a technique. The idea of grilling the tomatoes until well charred and reducing the base without burning probably sounds ridiculous. I mean how could you "burn" a soup with blackened tomatoes?! But hey, it's true. Consequently, the base should be constantly stirred to prevent the bottom from burning.

—€ The cream should be added at the end and only reheated. Long term simmering can cause the heavy cream to separate and the soup to taste old.

—€ The early and constant seasoning and tasting of the soup is extremely important in this and all quality cooking.

Technically speaking Michigan's thumb refers to the three counties of Huron, Sanilac and Tuscola, all three nicely tucked into the geographic digit on the east coast of the mitt. Settled mostly by Polish and German immigrants it's also referred to as our green thumb for its fertile farmland and rich agricultural roots. Home to Sebewaing, the sugar beet capitol of the world, it's also home to Kinde which was once hailed as the bean capitol. Even though Kinde lost its crown, the thumb grows more beans than any place else in the nation. With our twelve commercial classes of beans it's the navy variety that tops the list with more than half of our production going to that lovely legume.

The Thumb

Michigan's beans are so popular that the US senate restaurant has had a Michigan Bean soup on the daily menu for ages. Surprisingly enough, it is said that Michigan black beans are mainly exported to Mexico and that 90% of Michigan cranberry beans are exported mainly to Italy, Spain, Portugal and Columbia. Then there's Bad Axe, which has been said to have derived its name from the broken axe that was found in the knot of a tree at the center of the city's crossroads. Beef cattle production is Michigan's fourth largest agricultural business and cattle are raised in just about every county in the mitt with the thumb having the largest percentage.

Cheese Fondue with Hard Apple Cider

lace the cider in a small non-reactive saucepan with the Emmenthaler, Gruyere,
oasted Garlic Purée, nutmeg, salt and pepper. Place over a high flame and bring to
boil. When the cheese is melted immediately add the slurry whisking briskly until
he fondue starts to thicken. As soon as the fondue is thick and smooth immediately
our into a serving crock and serve with the cubed bread.

ecommended beverage: Misteguay Hard Apple Cider

Serves 2–4 as an appetizer

8 ounces hard apple cider, preferably from Michigan

8 ounces Emmenthaler cheese, grated

8 ounces Gruyere, grated

1 tablespoon Roasted Garlic Purée, page 88

1 pinch nutmeg

1 pinch sea salt

1 pinch black pepper, freshly ground, or to taste

1 ounce unbleached all-purpose flour slurry, (equal parts cold water and flour mixed until smooth)

3 cups cubed crusty day old artisan bread

Fondue translates from French o English as "melted", so then a clasic fondue au fromage would be "meltd cheese"—sounds better in French oesn't it?!

Surprisingly enough, earlier ecipes for fondue that I came across ll have the same ingredients that ne would find nowadays at restaurants all through Europe, save one major addition, a slurry. A slurry is food-speak for equal parts cold liquid, usually water combined with a starch, usually wheat flour, that have been thoroughly mixed to form, well a slurry-like mixture used to homogenize and thicken the fondue. Yes, before the advent of the slurry all fondues were just that, melted cheese!

Barbecue Beef Brisket

Serves 10–12

one 7–8 pound whole beef brisket, trimmed

½ recipe Basic Barbecue Rub, page 127

18 ounces ballpark mustard

1 gallon beef broth

2 whole onions, peeled and halved

6 whole carrots, split

6 ribs celery, split

6 hardnecked garlic heads

12 bay leaves

8 cups hickory chips, soaked and drained

Using a sprinkle jar or by hand, lightly dust the beef brisket with half of the rub. Using a pastry brush give the rubbed beef brisket a thorough coating of the mustard. Using the remaining rub dust the entire mustard coated brisket.

PREPARE 2 HICKORY-CHIP "PILLOWS" AS FOLLOWS

Place the drained wood chips in the center of an 18-inch square of heavy-duty aluminum foil. Fold all four sides of foil in, to encase the chips creating a "pillow." Repeat the procedure placing the pillow in the center of another square of foil and seal. Turn the double sealed pillow over and with a sharp utility knife cut 4 to 6 holes about the size of a quarter evenly spaced on the surface of the foil to allow the smoke to escape during cooking.

Place the hickory-chip pillow on the primary burner of a gas grill. Turn all of the burners to high heat with the lid down and cook until the chips start smoking heavily, about 10 to 20 minutes. Turn the primary burner down to medium-low and turn the rest of the burners off.

Peel the outermost layers of skin off the heads of garlic leaving an intact whole head free of any scrap. Split the heads in half cutting across the equator opening the cloves.

Place the seasoned brisket fat side up directly on the grill grate over a disposable foil pan filled halfway with beef broth, onions, carrots, celery, garlic and bay leaves on the unlit burner and close the lid.

After two hours replace the first hickory-chip pillow with a fresh one and top off the beef broth pan and continue to check and top off as needed every hour or so.

Cook the brisket for a total of 12 to 16 hours regulating the heat between 220 and 250 degrees F. The wide variance in cooking times is due in part to the varying size of the beef briskets, the grill/smoker setup, the fuel, the ambient temperature outside and how you like it cooked.

When the brisket is tender the beef is done. Carefully remove the barbecued brisket from the grill and let it rest for at least 30 minutes loosely covered with foil.

While the brisket is resting strain the smoked beef broth into a suitable size saucepan discarding the vegetables and top off with any remaining broth. Over a medium-high heat reduce the broth to a sauce-like consistency.

Slice brisket against the grain and serve on a platter with reduced sauce on the side.

Recommended beverage: Peninsula Cellars Cabernet/Merlot

Basic Barbecue Rub

Combine all the ingredients in a mixing bowl and blend well.

Makes about 4 cups

1 cup sea salt

½ cup maple sugar, preferably from Michigan

½ cup ancho chile powder

1 tablespoon aji amarillo powder

¼ cup black pepper, freshly ground, or to taste

½ cup smoked paprika powder

½ cup roasted garlic powder

¼ cup cumin powder

¼ cup dry mustard powder

¼ cup dried mixed herbs

⊸ This makes enough rub for two briskets. Can be scaled up or down as needed.

⊸ Olive oil can be added to the dry rub to transform it into a wet marinade. Simply whisk in the desired amount of olive oil until a thick paste forms. Use as you would the dry rub for a different effect.

⊸ Store the rub in a sealed container preferably away from heat and light in cook dark pantry or freezer. The blend will keep for several months.

unkle e's ramblings on 'cuing!

Although it may seem a bit Nouveau-trailer-park, the addition of America's premier ballpark mustard is an intriguing addition to beef brisket or pork/beef ribs. Numerous championship 'cuers swear by the initial mustard rub as their secret weapon. The idea of coating the beef in mustard is not unlike the liberal use of mustard in the French classic "lapin aux moutarde". The mustard seems to have three benefits. The first offers a crispy-end-crust by acting as a culinary glue to hold the smoking rub in place, the second, as a mild flavor enhancer that mellows during the long cooking time, and the third, as a tenderizer. It is reasoned that the high vinegar content of the mustard actually tenderizes the meat during the prolonged cooking.

The idea for doneness is not just a matter of being cooked through. The meat was cooked probably after 4 hours. What we are looking for here is more than doneness but tenderness. Brisket, being by definition the breast of the cow directly behind the fore legs is an extremely tough cut. What we are looking for is breaking down the marbling in the center of the meat, allowing the muscle bundles to break down achieving tenderness. The best method for achieving these results is low heat over a long period of time. As we northerners say "smoking" or the southerners say "barbeques" it's the extremely low heat and long cooking time that achieves our goal.

Chilled Spelt, Sweet Corn and Tomato Salad

Serves 4

1 cup whole spelt, preferably from Michigan

2 ears sweet corn, preferably from Michigan, cooked and cooled

16 whole cherry tomatoes, preferably from Michigan, quartered

4 teaspoons fresh oregano, chopped

4 teaspoons fresh thyme, chopped

2 tablespoons fresh chives, chopped

¼ cup slivered almonds, toasted

2 tablespoons extra virgin cold pressed olive oil

4 teaspoons white wine vinegar

sea salt, to taste

black pepper, freshly ground, to taste

Place spelt in a small bowl with water to cover. Cover with plastic wrap, and let rest overnight on countertop. When ready to cook, drain spelt, and place in a small pan with water to cover. Bring to a boil, and cook for about 10 minutes, until tender.

Scrape kernels from corncob, and place in a bowl large enough to hold all ingredients. Add remaining ingredients, and mix well. When spelt is cooked, drain well and toss with other ingredients while still warm.

It is best served at room temperature but can be chilled.

Recommended beverage: Bel Lago Pinot Grigio

In ancient Rome it was known as "farrum," the current Italians prize it as "farro," our German friends named it "dinkle," (I love that! dinkle—hahahaha) and origins can be traced back to early Mesopotamia. Now here in the mitt it goes by the name spelt or as the eggheads would say "triticum spelta" which is an ancient and distant cousin to today's modern wheat. Spelt is one of the oldest cultivated grains and prized for its nutty rich flavor. But it's not just good taste that has caught the culinary conscience of consumers on this side of the Atlantic. The grain is naturally high in fiber and contains significantly more protein than wheat. Spelt is also higher in B complex vitamins and both simple and complex carbohydrates. Another important benefit is that some gluten-sensitive gastronauts have been able to include spelt-based foods in their diets! Try some topped with a nice piece of pan seared lake fish or as a side dish as part of a larger buffet.

Lake Effect Jumbo Sea Scallops with Hard Apple Cider Butter Sauce

In a medium, heavy bottomed non-stick pan heat the olive oil over medium-high heat until it ripples.

Dust the scallops with the Lake Effect Seasoning and carefully add to the pan.

Cook quickly each side until golden brown, about 1 to 2 minutes per side.

Remove from the heat and serve immediately with the Hard Apple Cider Butter Sauce.

Recommended beverage: Chateau Grand Traverse Pinot Gris Dry

Serves 4

2 tablespoons extra virgin cold pressed olive oil

¼ cup Lake Effect Seasoning, page 188

8 jumbo sea scallops, dry packed "diver"

1 cup Hard Apple Cider Butter Sauce, page 132

unkle e's ramblings on scallops!

What's a diver scallop? Well, scallops unlike their culinary cousins oysters and mussels differ in many ways, but where the other two are sedentary the scallop likes to move about. They open their thin, round shells and suck in water to flitter about the sea floor. So gastronomically speaking they can get quite sandy from all that exercise. Hmmm, so where does that leave us? Oh yeah, "diver." Well, most scallops are dredged; meaning large underwater rakes are pulled along the sea bottom by powerful boats dragging the poor scallops. They eventually get filled full of sand, crushed from the constant pull of the rake and die. Yikes! What a watery way to go! But, "diver" scallops are actually hand picked by human divers so you get perfectly picked scallops that have no excess sand blasted into their succulent sweet flesh and are in perfect health—the only way to go!

All butter sauces have the disadvantage of "breaking" which is to say the butter solids break from the butterfat resulting in an oily curdled ookey mess. One great way of keeping your butter sauce hot is placing the finished sauce in a quality thermos. The thermos will keep the sauce at a perfect temperature for hours so you can do this classically difficult sauce ahead of time with no worries.

Hard Apple Cider Butter Sauce

Makes about 2 cups

1 cup hard apple cider, preferably from Michigan

¼ cup fresh lemon juice

2 whole shallots, peeled and finely chopped

2 bay leaves

½ cup heavy cream (optional)

1 pound unsalted sweet butter, chilled and cubed

sea salt, to taste

Clancy's Fancy Hot Sauce, or similar, to taste

In a heavy bottomed 2-quart non-reactive saucepan, combine apple cider, lemon juice, shallots and bay leaves. Simmer over medium heat for 8 to 10 minutes until the mixture is reduced to a wet paste, about 2 tablespoons.

At this point you may add the optional cream.

Add the cream and continue to simmer until reduced again to about 2 tablespoons. (Cream is added to make the sauce more stable and less likely to separate.)

Reduce the heat to low and remove the bay leaves. Whisk in the cubes of butter in small batches. The butter should melt without the sauce getting too hot, producing a creamy emulsified sauce. Do not let the sauce go over 130 degrees F, where it will separate. If the sauce starts to break, remove from heat, add 2 ice cubes and whisk until it cools down and comes back together.

Season to taste with the salt and hot sauce. Strain through a fine mesh strainer, or a double fold of dampened cheesecloth.

Serve immediately. Keep covered in a warm place for a few hours, if needed.

Fromage Blanc

Makes about 1½ cups

8 cups Creamline milk (If Creamline milk is unavailable substitute 7 cups of the best quality whole milk available with the addition of 1-cup of heavy cream)

2 cups cultured buttermilk

2 tablespoons fresh lemon juice, strained

¼–½ tablespoon sea salt

In a large, heavy saucepan, add the Creamline milk.

In a mixing bowl, combine the buttermilk, lemon juice and salt. Stir to combine. Add the buttermilk-lemon juice mixture to the milk and begin to heat the milk over low heat and very slowly, to 175 degrees F.

While the milk is heating, gently stir twice, making 2 strokes each time, with a heatproof, non-reactive spatula or other flat utensil. Check the temperature often. As soon as the temperature reaches 175 degrees F, remove the pot from the heat and allow to sit, undisturbed, for 10 minutes.

Line a large colander with 2 layers of fine cheesecloth set over a large bowl. Gently ladle the curds and whey into the colander and allow to drain until the drips of whey slows, about 2 minutes. Tie the corners of the cheesecloth together to form a hanging pouch, and hang pouch over a bowl and allow to drain until the cheese reaches the desired consistency.

Refrigerate until ready to serve, up to 1 week. If cheese is marinated in oil with fresh herbs, it will keep, refrigerated, for up to 1 month.

Wood Roasted Great Northern White Bean "Hummus" with Two Garlics and Tahini

Preheat the oven to 450 degrees F.

In a medium saucepan over medium-high heat add some of the olive oil. Then immediately follow with the onions, fresh garlic and bay leaves and cook until the onions are soft, about 5 minutes.

Add the white beans and water and place in the oven, lightly tented with foil until the beans are very soft and the mixture is thick, about 20 to 30 minutes.

Remove the bay leaves and add a bit more of the olive oil, Roasted Garlic Purée, lemon juice and tahini in the bowl of a food processor fitted with a steel blade and process until smooth.

With the machine running, slowly add the olive oil until emulsified. Season with salt, pepper and hot sauce to taste.

Serve with artisan bread, Chowder Crackers (page 175) or similar.

Makes about 2 cups

½ cup extra virgin cold pressed olive oil

1 large red onion, peeled and cut julienne

3 cloves fresh hardnecked garlic

3 large bay leaves

3 cups great Northern white beans, cooked or canned, drained and rinsed

¼ cup fresh water

¼ cup Roasted Garlic Purée, page 88

1 cup fresh lemon juice

2 tablespoons tahini

sea salt, to taste

black pepper, freshly ground, to taste

Clancy's Fancy Hot Sauce, or similar, to taste

Michigan Inspired "Choucroute Garni"

Serves 10–12

3–4 pounds sauerkraut, fresh bulk, preferably not canned

12 tablespoons lard, or rendered bacon, chicken, duck or goose fat

1 pound Maple Cured Hickory Smoked Bacon, page 153, cut into large chunks

2 white onions, peeled and sliced

2 whole Honeycrisp apples, preferably from Michigan, or similar, peeled, cored and sliced

3 cups hard apple cider, preferably from Michigan

2 cup poultry stock or water

black pepper, freshly ground, to taste

6 whole cloves

6 juniper berries, or a bit of gin

2 bay leaves

¼ cup Roasted Garlic Purée, page 88

3 bratwurst, Koegels, or similar

3 Vienna frankfurters, Koegels, or similar

3 pounds smoked polish sausage, Koegels, or similar

1 pound ring bologna, Koegels, or similar

3 bockwurst, Koegels, or similar

2 pounds new potatoes

4 rashers Maple Cured Hickory Smoked Bacon, page 153

Preheat the oven to 350 degrees F.

Rinse the sauerkraut in a colander under cold running water. Taste after rinsing, and if it is still very acidic or salty, repeat several more times. Drain very well.

In a large casserole over low heat, melt the fat with the chunked bacon and add the onions and apples. Sauté until the onions and apples are wilted, then add the hard apple cider and stock or water.

Add the drained sauerkraut, pepper, cloves, juniper berries, and bay leaves and Roasted Garlic Purée. Blend well and cover and bake in the oven for 1 to 1½ hours.

In separate saucepans cook each variety of sausage in gently simmering water for about 20 minutes. Do not allow the water to boil or the sausages will burst. Drain all the sausages, slice the ring bologna, and keep it all warm until serving time.

Meanwhile, steam or boil the potatoes. Allow them to cool just enough to handle, then peel. Keep warm.

Just before serving, cook the bacon rashers until very crisp.

To serve, drain the sauerkraut—pick out all the herbs and spices—and mound it in the center of a large heated platter. Surround the sauerkraut with the sausages, the potatoes and the crisp bacon rashers. Serve with plenty of different kinds of mustard, quality breads, and plenty of chilled Michigan hard apple cider, wines and artisan beers.

I like to keep extra cider and or poultry broth handy just in case the choucroute dries out too quickly during cooking. Always check every quarter hour or so to make sure the choucroute is juicy, if not, add a bit more cider or broth.

The variety and amounts of sausages is really up to you. More people coming over for dinner than you thought? No problema! Add a few more of Flints finest.

Are they French or are they German? Alsace and Lorraine have changed nationality four times since 1871 alone and though these two provinces are now part of eastern France, they form a region where traditions mingle too closely to separate. The dictionary definition of choucroute translates simply as fermented cabbage, that hot dog condiment, sauerkraut. But no self respecting gastronome can forget the show stopping definitive dish of Alsace, "choucroute garni." This culinary classic finds the puckery cabbage drained and rinsed before its hours of cooking with mountains of onions, garlic, wine and of course, piles-o-pig!

Skirt Steak is the diaphragm muscle of cattle. This tasty cut of beef is woefully underused at home here in the USA but, is beginning to find a place on restaurant menus across the country judging by the recent price spike at the markets. Fajita literally translates to "sashes" because of the long thin shape of the meat, which has a very noticeable coarse grain. Even though the meat looks tough and ratty, properly prepared it is one of the tastiest cuts. There are two cuts of skirt steak available, the inner and the outer. I prefer the outer cut; it tends to be a bit larger, a bit tenderer and a bit more flavorful.

Skirt Steak Fajitas with Michigan Ale and Apple Cider Marinade

In a medium mixing bowl add all of the marinade ingredients and blend thoroughly. Add the skirt steak and submerge. Cover the bowl with plastic wrap and refrigerate. This should be done at least 2 hours before grilling or better yet the night before.

Preheat your wood burning or gas grill to medium-high heat according to the manufacturers directions.

Remove the skirt steak from the marinade and pat dry. In a small mixing bowl blend together all of the ingredients for the Maple Fajita Rub. Generously coat the steaks with rub and let sit for 30 minutes to "cure" the meat.

Grill the meat over a medium-high flame turning once for about 4 to 5 minutes, basting with the leftover marinade or until the meat is a very juicy medium rare. This particular cut of meat can be extremely thin and is difficult to cook to exact temperatures.

While the steaks are cooking preheat your griddle or sauté pan over medium-high heat. Add the olive oil and immediately add the onions. Sauté the onions for 2 to 3 minutes or until just wilted and add all of the peppers. Stir the peppers and onions to combine and season to taste with some of the Maple Fajita Rub and a drizzle of the reserved marinade. After about 5 minutes the onions and peppers should be wilted and soft. Toss in the chopped cilantro just to heat through, remove from heat and keep warm.

When the steaks are ready remove from the heat and let rest for 5 to 10 minutes. Cut the steaks across the grain (it makes for smaller slices but they will be far more tender).

To serve, mound the sliced skirt steak on a large platter along with the onions and peppers and pour over a bit of the reserved marinade and dust with the Maple Fajita Rub. Serve with the warmed flour tortillas, Hickory Smoked Tomato Salsa and Hickory Smoked Jalapeño Sour Cream, and avocado.

Recommended beverage: Crooked Tree Dark Horse IPA

Serves 8

FOR THE ALE APPLE MARINADE
12 ounces local artisan beer, preferably from Michigan

½ cup fresh apple cider, preferably from Michigan and unpasturized

3 whole limes, juiced

2 tablespoons Worcestershire sauce

2 tablespoons extra virgin cold pressed olive oil

two 1-pound outer skirt steaks

FOR MAPLE FAJITA RUB
2 tablespoons sea salt

2 tablespoon maple sugar, preferably from Michigan

4 tablespoons oregano, preferably Mexican

2 tablespoons ancho chile, powder

2 tablespoons cumin, powder

FOR THE MIXED VEGETABLES
2–4 tablespoons extra virgin cold pressed olive oil

1 large red onion, peeled and cut julienne

1 large red bell pepper, cut julienne

1 large yellow bell pepper, cut julienne

1 large green pepper, cut julienne

½ bunch fresh cilantro, coarsely chopped

FOR THE FAJITA GARNISHES
16 ounces Hickory Smoked Tomato Salsa, page 87

8 ounces Hickory Smoked Jalapeño Cream, page 184

1 large ripe avocado, sliced

8 large flour tortillas, warmed

Gluten-Free Cream Biscuits

Makes about 8–10

2 cups Heartlands Finest gluten-free performance blend flour, or similar

4 teaspoons baking powder

¼ teaspoon baking soda

¾ teaspoon sea salt

4 tablespoons lard, chilled

1½ cups heavy cream, chilled

FOR THE BISCUIT GLAZE (OPTIONAL)

2 tablespoons heavy cream

2 tablespoons unsalted sweet butter, melted

Preheat oven to 450 degrees F.

In a large mixing bowl, combine flour, baking powder, baking soda and salt. Using your fingertips or a pastry cutter, rub or cut the chilled lard into dry ingredients until mixture looks like crumbs. (The faster the better, you don't want the fats to melt.) Make a well in the center and pour in the chilled heavy cream. Stir just until the dough comes together. The dough will be very sticky.

Turn dough onto floured surface, dust top with flour and gently fold dough over on itself 2 or 3 times. Press into a 1-inch thick square. Cut out biscuits with large sharp chef's knife (that has been lightly floured), being sure to push straight down through the dough.

For softer biscuits place on baking sheet so that they just touch or with a ½-inch spread for crisper biscuits.

FOR THE BISCUIT GLAZE (OPTIONAL)

Combine the heavy cream and the unsalted butter in a small bowl and using a pasty brush gently glaze the tops of the biscuits.

Bake until biscuits are tall and light gold on top, 15 to 20 minutes.

unkle e's ramblings on biscuits!

Since biscuits cut from a second pass of the dough will not be quite as light as those from the first why on earth do we continually cut them in rounds? If the biscuits are cut into squares there is no reason for a second roll and all the biscuits will be the same size!

◄ A floured knife or pastry cutter gives a cleaner cut to the dough allowing the biscuit to rise higher than a dull cut.

◄ If you prefer a round biscuit use a round cutter but make sure it's well floured and you use an up and down motion when cutting the biscuit. Twisting the cutter can stretch the dough which could inhibit rising.

◄ Baking temperature on various biscuit recipes vary widely and what I have found out (not surprisingly) is a higher temperature produces a crisper darker biscuit where a lower temperature offers a lighter and softer biscuit.

◄ The biscuit glaze is optional but offers not only an unsurpassed richness and that special butter flavor but also results in a browned glossy top.

Maple Sage Breakfast Sausage

Makes about 2½ pounds of sausage

2 pounds pork butt, cut into ¼-inch pieces

½ pound Maple Cured Hickory Smoked Bacon, page 153, cut into ¼-inch pieces

2 teaspoons sea salt

1½ teaspoons black pepper, freshly ground

3–4 teaspoons fresh sage leaves, finely chopped

1 tablespoon maple sugar, preferably from Michigan

½ teaspoon fresh grated nutmeg

½ teaspoon red pepper flakes

Combine the pork with all other ingredients in a bowl and blend. Chill for at least 1 hour or preferably overnight.

Using the fine blade of a meat grinder, grind the pork mixture.

The bulk sausage at this point can be used as is or formed into 1-inch rounds or filled into sausage casings for links.

You can substitute pure pork fat or fat back in place of the raw bacon in this recipe. I have found using high quality smoked bacon gives the sausage a pleasant smoky flavor without the added steps of cold smoking the sausage.

Maple Sage Sausage "Gluten-Free" Gravy

In a heavy skillet over medium-high heat place the sausage. (I prefer a well-seasoned cast iron skillet for this dish but any heavy bottomed skillet would be fine.) Cook the sausage for about 7 minutes while breaking it up with a wooden spoon. When all of the sausage is cooked and you have achieved a nice browned crust carefully remove the sausage from the pan with a slotted spoon to a bowl and set aside.

Remove and discard all but 2 to 3 tablespoons of sausage fat from the skillet.

Over medium heat, stir the gluten-free flour into the fat. Stir constantly until browned, about 5 minutes.

Pour the 2 cups of the milk into the skillet stirring constantly to blend taking care to release the browned "kibbles n'bits" from the bottom of the pan. Those bits of caramelized pork, all full of flavor will help to flavor the gravy. Season to taste with salt and pepper. Add the sausage back into the skillet with the parsley and bring to a simmer for about 2 minutes. If the gravy is a bit too thick for your liking after adding the sausage, you can thin it out with the remainder of the milk.

TO SERVE

Split the biscuits in half and divide them among plates. Top the bottoms of the split biscuits with some of the gravy and replace the tops. Spoon a bit more gravy over all and serve immediately.

Makes about 3 cups gravy

1 pound Maple Sage Breakfast Sausage, page 140

4 tablespoons Heartlands Finest gluten-free performance blend flour, or similar

2–3 cups whole milk

¼ cup flat parsley leaves, chopped

sea salt, to taste

black pepper, freshly ground, to taste

Gluten-Free Cream Biscuits, page 138

You can adjust the thickness of the gravy by increasing the amount of milk, adding little by little until you get the consistency you like. Keep in mind if you do that recheck for seasoning.

If for some reason the sausage doesn't yield enough fat during browning simply add enough lard (or olive oil, butter etc.) to make up the difference when making the roux.

Grilled New York Strip Steaks with Coffee Chili Rub

Preheat your grill.

Rub the meat well with 1 teaspoon salt, pepper, and olive oil.

Combine the ground coffee, aji amarillo powder, cocoa powder, cinnamon and mix well.

Spread the mixture over a work surface and coat each steak in it until coated evenly. Allow to marinate approximately 30 minutes at room temperature.

Grill the steaks over medium-high heat turning only once to desired doneness.

Check the beef's internal temperature with a meat thermometer (125 degrees F for medium-rare, 135 degrees F for medium).

Remove the steaks from the grill and let rest for a few minutes before serving.

Recommended beverage: Renaissance Cellars Cabernet Franc

— Dry rub can be scaled up or down as needed.

— Olive oil can be added to the dry rub to transform it into a wet marinade. Simply whisk in the desired amount of olive oil until a thick paste forms. Use as you would the dry rub for a different effect.

— Store the rub in a sealed container preferably away from heat and light in cook dark pantry or freezer. The blend will keep for several months.

— If you are hankering for a bit more caffeine, serve this steak with the Coffee Maple Glaze, page 185, for an extra jolt!

Serves 4

four 12-ounce New York steaks, trimmed

2 teaspoons sea salt

½ teaspoon black pepper, freshly ground, or to taste

2 tablespoons extra virgin cold pressed olive oil

FOR COFFEE CHILI RUB

2 tablespoons coffee beans, fresh and finely ground

1 tablespoon cocoa powder, unsweetened

1 teaspoon aji amarillo powder, or similar

⅛ teaspoon Saigon cinnamon, freshly ground

Michigan Steamed Brown Bread with Dried Cherries and Walnuts

Makes 3 loaves

1 cup rye flour, preferably from Michigan

1 cup whole wheat flour, preferably from Michigan

1 cup cornmeal, preferably from Michigan, coarse grind, yellow or white

2 teaspoons baking soda

1 teaspoon sea salt

¾ cup maple syrup, preferably from Michigan

2 cups cultured buttermilk

1 cup dried tart cherries, preferably from Michigan

¾ cup coarsely chopped walnuts

Preheat your oven to 350 degrees F.

In a large bowl mix together dry ingredients. Stir in remaining wet ingredients, cherries and nuts until just combined.

STEAMED JAR/CAN METHOD (MAKES A MOIST BREAD)

Prepare the three, 21-ounce French styled jelly jars (oven-proof) or comparable sized cans with butter or pan spray followed by a light dusting of flour.

Pour the batter evenly into the 3 jars about ⅔ full, covered tightly with foil (leaving a 1-inch gap of head room on top for bread expansion). Tie with cotton kitchen twine and place in a suitable high sided stockpot. Pour in boiling water about halfway up the sides of the jars and cover with a lid. Bake in the middle of the oven until a tester comes out clean, about one hour (keep your eyes on the water level and replenish if needed).

Carefully, remove the jars from the water and cool bread in the jars for 10 to 15 minutes. Carefully turn loaves out onto a rack and cool completely before slicing.

BAKED LOAF PAN METHOD (MAKES A DRIER BREAD LOAF)

Prepare a standard loaf pan (9¼ x 5¼ x 2¾-inches) with butter or pan spray followed by a light dusting of flour.

Pour batter into prepared pan and bake in middle of oven until a tester comes out clean, about 1 hour.

Cool bread in pan on a rack for 5 minutes. Turn loaf out onto rack and cool completely before slicing.

This bread is a variation of the classic steamed brown bread of Boston. By regionalizing the ingredients with maple syrup and tart dried cherries I felt it was a fitting tribute to the original.

Baked Michigan Navy Beans with Smoked Bacon, Chiles and Cocoa

Serves 10–12

1 pound navy beans, picked over, rinsed and soaked overnight in cold water, preferably from Michigan

6 cups cold water, plus ½ cup boiling water

1 large pasilla chile, whole

¼ cup lard

2 large red onions, peeled and diced

1 pound Maple Cured Hickory Smoked Bacon, chopped, page 153, or similar

¼ teaspoon chipotle chili powder

¾ cup maple sugar, preferably from Michigan

½ cup Roasted Garlic Purée, page 88

¼ teaspoon nutmeg, ground

¼ teaspoon cloves, ground

¼ teaspoon cumin, ground

¼ teaspoon sweet paprika, ground

⅓ cup tomato paste

1¼ cups stout beer, preferably from Michigan

3 cups poultry broth, or similar to finish the beans

2 ounces cocoa powder, unsweetened

1½ teaspoons sea salt, or to taste

½ teaspoons black pepper, freshly ground, or to taste

Preheat your oven to 350 degrees F.

Drain and rinse the soaked beans. In a large saucepan, cover the beans with 6 cups of the water and bring to a boil. Reduce the heat to low, cover and simmer until tender, anywhere from 30 minutes to 1 hour. You want the beans tender but not falling apart.

Meanwhile, soak the pasilla in the ½-cup of the boiling water until softened, about 20 minutes. Drain the pasilla. Discard the stem, seeds and water, mince the chile.

In a large, heavy bottomed casserole or bean pot heat the lard. Add the onion and cook over moderate heat until softened, about 2 to 3 minutes.

Add the bacon and cook until softened, 2 to 3 minutes longer. Stir in the minced pasilla, chipotle powder, maple sugar, Roasted Garlic Purée, nutmeg, cloves, cumin, paprika and tomato paste into the bacon and toast the ingredients a bit to intensify the flavors for another 2 to 3 minutes.

Top off with the beer and the broth.

Drain the navy beans and add them to the casserole, stir to blend.

Cover and place the casserole in the preheated oven until the sauce has thickened, about 1 hour. If you like your beans thicker remove the cover after 30 minutes.

Taste the beans and adjust seasonings. Stir in the cocoa powder, season with salt and pepper and serve.

Maple Corndogs

Heat oil in a deep fryer to 365 degrees F.

In a large bowl, stir together the flour, cornmeal, maple sugar, baking powder, aji amarillo powder and salt. Make a well in the center, and pour in the egg, Roasted Garlic Purée, melted bacon drippings (optional), buttermilk and baking soda. Mix until everything is smooth and well blended.

FOR THE TRADITIONAL CORNDOG

Place the cornstarch onto a cookie sheet. Gently shake the pan back and forth to disperse the starch. Roll each hot dog in the cornstarch and shake to remove any excess.

Fill a large drinking glass three-quarters to the top with the batter (refill the glass as needed). Insert wooden sticks into the ends of the hot dogs and quickly dip in and out of the batter shaking off any excess. Immediately and carefully place each hot dog into the hot oil, and cook until coating is golden brown, about 4 to 5 minutes. With tongs, remove to cooling rack, and allow to drain for 3 to 5 minutes.

FOR AN "OCTOPUS" CORNDOG

Cut hot dog in half, lengthwise, leaving about 2" intact at the end. Cut each of the long sections in half (lengthwise), then in half again. These will be the octopus legs. Carefully roll each hot dog in the cornstarch making sure to get in between the legs and shake to remove any excess.

Fill a large drinking glass three-quarters to the top with the batter (refill the glass as needed). Insert wooden sticks into the ends of the hot dogs and quickly dip in and out of the batter shaking off any excess being careful to get batter in between the legs. Immediately and carefully spread the legs a bit to prevent sticking them together and slowly place each hot dog into the hot oil, gently swinging them back and forth allowing the legs to curl and cook until coating is golden brown, about 4 to 5 minutes. With tongs, remove to cooling rack, and allow to drain standing up for 3 to 5 minutes. The kulinary kiddies love these!!

Serve with ballpark style mustard.

Serves 6–6

1 quart soybean oil, for deep frying, preferably from Michigan

wooden sticks, for the hot dogs

1 cup unbleached all-purpose flour, preferably from Michigan

⅔ cup yellow cornmeal, preferably from Michigan

¼ cup maple sugar, preferably from Michigan

1½ teaspoons baking powder

½ tablespoon aji amarillo powder

1 teaspoon sea salt

1 large egg, beaten

2 tablespoons Roasted Garlic Purée, page 88

1 tablespoon bacon drippings, optional

1¼ cups cultured buttermilk

½ teaspoon baking soda

¼ cup cornstarch

2 pounds hot dogs, Koegels or similar

Grilled Romaine Salad with Smoked Tomatoes, Maytag Blue and Maple Spiced Nuts

Preheat your gas or wood-burning grill as per the manufacturers directions.

Rub the cut sides of the lettuce with a bit of the Smoked Tomato Vinaigrette.

Place the lettuce cut side down on the grill and cook 3 to 4 minutes or until the lettuce is slightly charred and warmed through.

Place the lettuce grilled side up on serving plates and top with the Smoked Tomato Vinaigrette following with the Maple Spice Nuts and cheese.

Serve immediately.

Serves 2

1 large romaine lettuce head, cleaned, trimmed and spit head to core

½ cup Smoked Tomato Vinaigrette, page 182

¼ cup Maple Rosemary Roasted Spice Nuts, recipe below

¼ cup Maytag Blue cheese, crumbled

Maple Rosemary Roasted Spiced Nuts

Preheat your oven to 350 degrees F.

Toss the nuts in a large bowl to combine and spread them out on a cookie sheet. Toast them in the oven until they become a light golden brown, about 10 to 15 minutes.

In the same large bowl, combine the rosemary, aji amarillo, maple sugar, salt and melted butter. Add the hot nuts directly to the bowl and toss well.

Pour the seasoned nuts back onto the cookie sheet, spread them out and let them cool.

Store in an airtight container.

Recommended beverage: Chateau Chantal Late Harvest Riesling

Makes about 1 ¼ pounds

1¼ pounds assorted nuts (peanuts, cashews, brazil nuts, hazelnuts, walnuts, pecans, whole unpeeled almonds)

4 tablespoons fresh rosemary, chopped

2 teaspoons aji amarillo powder

4 teaspoons maple sugar, preferably from Michigan

4 teaspoons sea salt

2 tablespoons unsalted sweet butter, melted

S ometimes forgotten with all the hoopla surrounding downstate, Michigan's upper peninsula is large. Take Connecticut, Delaware, Massachusetts and Rhode Island, stir them up in a huge mixing bowl and The U.P. is still bigger. Even though it contains almost one-third of the land area of the mitten it only has 3% of the population. Though we are all Michiganders, residents of the land above the bridge are frequently called Yoopers and wear their regional identity proudly. Described as a "sterile region on the shores of Lake Superior destined by soil and climate to remain forever a wilderness" by the US Congress, in 1837 copper mining changed everything. Initially not profitable because of transportation issues, the opening of the Soo Locks and the docks in Marquette allowed the U.P. to eventually produce more mineral wealth than the California Gold Rush. By 1960, 90% of all America's copper came from

The U.P.

that "sterile region." The last copper mine closed in 1965 but the culinary influence of the Cornish miners lives on in what has been called U.P. soul food — the beef pasty. The Finns have their own version of the pasty and have greatly contributed to the culinary landscape with old world classics like *nisu*, a cardamom-flavored sweet bread; *pannukakku*, a variant on the pancake with a custard flavor; *viili* (sometimes spelled "fellia"), a stretchy, fermented Finnish milk; and *korppu*, hard slices of toasted cinnamon-bread, traditionally dipped in coffee. One Italian dish of note is something called *cudighi* even though the word is not found in Italy it can be found all over the U.P. A spicy sausage flavored with clove and cinnamon, it can be served on its own or in a sandwich paired with mozzarella cheese and tomato sauce.

Maple Cured Hickory Smoked Bacon

In a mixing bowl, blend the sugar, salt, pepper and thyme together.

Place a large piece of plastic wrap (at least twice the size of the pork belly) on your workspace. Spread half of the Maple Cure in the center of the plastic wrap and place the pork belly over top. Shake the remaining cure over the top of the pork making sure to cover it all and wrap the pork belly tightly in the plastic wrap. Wrap the belly one more time with another piece of plastic wrap.

Cure the belly in the wrap for 36 hours under refrigeration. Remove from the refrigerator, unwrap the pork and rinse off the cure. Pat the pork dry.

Place the cured pork belly (fat side up) in a smoker and following the manufacturers directions, add the drained hickory chips and "cold smoke" the belly for 12 to 16 hours.

Refrigerate and or freeze the bacon and use as needed.

Makes 10 pounds

10 pounds fresh pork belly, skinned

3 cups hickory chips, soaked in water and drained

FOR THE MAPLE CURE
1 cup maple sugar, preferably from Michigan

1 cup sea salt

¼ cup black pepper, freshly ground, or to taste

¼ cup dried thyme

unkle e's ramblings
on bacon!

Ahhh, bacon—this perfect porcine product has to be one of—if not my favorite—foods! So here's the deal on American bacon—it's traditionally made from pork bellies that have been cured or brined with traditional seasonings like sugar and salt then cold smoked over some flavorful wood. Simple, eh? But, like all good things somewhere along the line an American breakfast icon lost its way. Corporate culinary giants got hold of my prized pig and started injecting the beautiful bellies with corn syrup, liquid smoke, nitrites, nitrates and a host of other incredible inedibles. So how can we return to what made American bacon the envy of all pig producing peoples? Well, the nitrate nitrite thing was truly important for long term storage and preserving that wonderful rosy color—but heck, how long do you plan on keeping bacon? Keep in mind in the new millennium we have "freezers," and we aren't preserving pork bellies as much as we are using that classic smoking technique to flavor the flesh! So do yourself a favor and put aside some time and try curing your own bellies and bring home the bacon!

French Styled Gnocchi with Exotic Mushrooms

Serves 4

3 tablespoons extra virgin cold pressed olive oil

¼ cup crimini mushrooms, trimmed, cut into wedges

¼ cup porcini or chanterelle mushrooms, trimmed, cut into wedges

¼ cup shiitake mushrooms, trimmed, cut into wedges

¼ cup button mushrooms, trimmed, cut into wedges

¼ cup oyster mushrooms, trimmed, cut into wedges

1 whole shallot, peeled and chopped

1 tablespoon Roasted Garlic Purée, page 88

½ cup semi-dry white wine, preferably from Michigan

1 quart Mushroom Broth, page 172

¼ cup crème fraîche or sour cream

¼ teaspoon fresh sage, chopped

1 pound French Style Gnocchi, cooked, page 155

sea salt, to taste

black pepper, freshly ground, to taste

1 tablespoon unsalted sweet butter

1 tablespoon Wisantigo Parmesan, or similar, grated

In a large, heavy bottomed non-reactive saucepan heat olive oil over high heat until sizzling and sauté the mushrooms until tender, about 3 to 4 minutes.

Lower heat and add shallots and Roasted Garlic Purée with the wine and reduce by half. Add the Mushroom Broth and bring to boil. Add crème fraîche and sage and let the mixture simmer for about 5 to 10 minutes or until the sauce is thick and creamy. Add the Gnocchi and toss until warmed through. Season to taste with the salt and pepper.

Right before you're ready to serve, swirl in the butter and garnish with the Parmesan cheese.

Recommended beverage: Shady Lane Pinot Noir

The origins of gnocchi's (nyoh-kee) name are a bit disheartening. The fact is, "gnocco" means "stupid person" or "blockhead," referring to the people who made uninspired dishes of dumplings without any flavor or sauce. With as many recipes for gnocchi as there are Italians I decided to offer you a recipe from the other side of the tracks—France. Even though gnocchi is considered a culinary icon of da boot, the French came up with a pretty kewl version of their own based on wheat flour, not the more popular potato. These luscious lumps of love are addictive! I have them paired here with Michigan morels but any sauce; even browned butter with a bit of cheese would be delicious!

French Style Gnocchi

Combine the salt, pepper, nutmeg, butter, and the water in a medium heavy bottomed saucepan. Bring to boil over high heat, stirring continuously with a large spoon.

Quickly remove the pan from the heat and add all of the flour at once. Beat vigorously with a large spoon to create a smooth dough. Reheat for 30 seconds to one minute over medium heat, stirring all the time, to allow the dough to dry out just a bit.

Quickly transfer the dough to the bowl of an electric mixer (or by hand). After about 5 to 10 minutes (or until the mixture has cooled a bit) add the Parmesan and 1 of the eggs. Mix at low speed (or by hand) until the eggs and cheese are thoroughly incorporated into the dough. Add the second egg and mix again until smooth. Finally add the third egg and mix until smooth. Cover the mixture with a bit of plastic wrap and let cool.

Bring a large wide mouthed saucepan filled with nicely salted water to about 180 degrees F or to a simmer.

Spoon the dough into a pastry bag fitted with a 1-inch plain tip. Let the tip rest on the edge of the saucepan and slowly squeeze the mixture out, cutting at the tip with a sharp knife or kitchen shears at 1½-inch intervals so they drop in the water.

Cook the gnocchi at a slow simmer, stirring occasionally, until they start to puff, about 5 minutes. They should resemble floating corks. To test for doneness, remove a dumpling and cut in half. The center should have tiny holes. With a slotted spoon, transfer gnocchi to a bowl of iced water to chill. Drain well in a colander.

Serves 4

1 teaspoon sea salt, or to taste

½ teaspoon black pepper, freshly ground, or to taste

½ teaspoon nutmeg, grated

2 tablespoons unsalted sweet butter

1 cup water

1 cup unbleached all-purpose flour

3 large egg yolks

¼ cup Wisantigo Parmesan, or similar, grated

salted water for poaching the gnocchi

Hickory Smoked Tomato Cocktail Sauce

Makes 2 cups

1½ cups Hickory Smoked Tomato Salsa, page 87

2–3 tablespoons, or to taste, prepared horseradish

½ cup ketchup

In a large non-reactive mixing bowl add the tomato salsa, horseradish and ketchup. Blend well.

Can be refrigerated 3 to 5 days.

Michigan Maple Pizza Dough

Makes four, 6 ounce balls

1 package active dry yeast

1 tablespoon maple syrup, preferably from Michigan

1 cup warm water, 105 to 115 degrees F

1½ cups unbleached all-purpose flour, plus additional for dusting, preferably from Michigan

1½ cups unbleached high gluten bread flour, preferably from Michigan

1 teaspoon sea salt

1 tablespoon extra virgin cold pressed olive oil, plus additional for brushing

2–4 tablespoons cornmeal, preferably from Michigan, coarse ground, for stretching pizzas

In a small bowl, dissolve the yeast and syrup in ¼-cup warm water.

In a mixer fitted with a dough hook, combine both flours and the sea salt. Add the oil, the yeast mixture, and the remaining ¾-cup of water and mix on low speed until the dough comes cleanly away from the sides of the bowl and clusters around the dough hook, about 5 minutes. (The pizza dough can also be made in a food processor fitted with the steel blade. Pulse once or twice, add the remaining ingredients, and process until the dough begins to form a ball.)

Turn the dough out onto a clean work surface and knead by hand 2 or 3 minutes longer. The dough should be smooth and firm. Cover the dough with a clean, damp towel and let it rise in a warm spot for about 30 minutes. (When ready, the dough will stretch as it is lightly pulled).

Divide the dough into 4 balls, about 6 ounces each. Work each ball by pulling down the sides and tucking under the bottom of the ball. Repeat 4 or 5 times. Then on a smooth, clean surface, roll the ball under the palm of your hand until the top of the dough is smooth and firm, about 1 minute. Cover the dough with a damp towel and let rest 15 to 20 minutes. At this point, the balls can be wrapped in plastic and refrigerated for up to 2 days.

Michigan Maple Spice Rub

Mix all the ingredients together in bowl.

Can be scaled up or down as needed.

Olive oil can be added to the dry rub to transform it into a wet marinade. Simply whisk in the desired amount of olive oil until a thick paste forms. Use as you would the dry rub for a different effect.

Store the rub in a sealed container preferably away from heat and light in cook dark pantry or freezer. The blend will keep for several months.

Makes about 2¼ cups

½ cup maple sugar, preferably from Michigan

½ cup paprika

½ cup roasted garlic powder

¼ cup ground cumin

¼ cup dry mustard powder

¼ cup black pepper, freshly ground, or to taste

¼ cup ancho chile powder

¼ cup dried thyme

1 cup sea salt

BLOCK HOUSE AND VILLAGE, MACKINAC ISLAND

Midwestern Risotto of Carnaroli and Great Lakes Wild Rice with Morel Mushrooms and White Truffle Oil

Serves 6

8–10 cups vegetable broth

6 tablespoons extra virgin cold pressed olive oil

2 large white onions, peeled and finely diced

sea salt, to taste

black pepper, freshly ground, to taste

Clancy's Fancy Hot Sauce, or similar, to taste

2 cups carnaroli rice

1 cup dried morel mushrooms, reconstituted in water and water reserved

1½ cups dry white wine, preferably from Michigan

½ cup Roasted Garlic Purée, page 88

½ cup Great Lakes wild rice, cooked, water reserved

6–8 tablespoons Compound Butter, page 178 (add black truffles per recipe instructions)

¾–1 cup Wisantigo Parmesan, grated

white truffle oil, to taste

In a large heavy bottomed stockpot over high heat bring vegetable broth to a boil; reduce heat and cover, keeping it ready stove-side.

In a large, heavy bottomed non-reactive sauté pan, heat the olive oil over low heat and "sweat" the onions until translucent, about 3 to 5 minutes. Begin light seasoning with the salt, pepper and hot sauce.

Increase the heat to medium-high and add the carnaroli rice, continue the sauté until the rice is well coated with the oil and the grains are slightly toasted, stirring with a wooden spoon, about 5 to 8 minutes (A wooden spoon is always preferable when making risotto, as a metal spoon tends to cut or injure the grains of rice).

Once the rice is toasted, add the morel mushrooms and follow with the white wine.

After the rice has absorbed the white wine and the skillet is nearly dry, begin adding the hot vegetable broth one cup at a time, stirring constantly and letting each addition be absorbed before adding the next, until the rice is tender and creamy looking but still al dente, about 18 to 20 minutes total (There may be broth left over).

Adding the liquid in stages, instead of all at once, allows the grains of rice to expand more fully, adding to the risotto's creamy texture.

Halfway through the cooking process add the Roasted Garlic Purée and continue with the light seasoning of salt, pepper and hot sauce to taste.

Remove the pan from heat and stir in the cooked wild rice, truffle butter and Parmesan until butter and cheese have melted. Taste and season if necessary, with salt, pepper, and hot sauce.

Pour into serving bowls and garnish with a bit more shaved Parmesan and drizzle over the truffle oil.

Serve immediately.

Recommended beverage: Brys Estate Pinot Grigio

In my attempt to put a Great Lakes face on risotto I was faced with a major dilemma, how does one replace the classic superfini's of Italy and if one does, what can be used that could even hold a candle to the classic? Then, of course, there is always the nagging question that lurks underneath the surface; when is change, just for changes sake?

Then one day it just came, Great Lakes wild rice.

At one point early in our history the native Americans that settled throughout the Great Lakes paddled for wild rice. Not a true rice at all, wild rice, is considered by the eggheads as an aquatic grass and consequently doesn't share any of its Italian cousins culinary attributes, so what's the point? Well, the point or punto (as my momma used to say) my dear culinarians is to use the addition of Great Lakes wild rice as a companion to the Italian superfini not as a replacement. Much like adding carrots or celery. What this does is add a unique and woodsy flavor to the finished risotto as well and if your timing is a bit off or if you, like myself like your risotto a bit less "al dente" than the young culinary bucks back in the kitchen, the addition of the firm cooked wild rice offers a safety net, adding a bit of al dente to your softer richly flavored superfino.

In Italian riso stands for rice and otto, well, I don't know what the hell otto means but if you put the two together you have one of the classic rice dishes of Italy—risotto. Historically this luscious rice dish gets its creamy consistency, surprisingly, not from cream but from the rice. Arborio, Carnaroli and Villa Nano rices are categorized as superfini and are characterized by their big round grains. These superfini are necessary, when combined with the constant heat from the range, the hot broth added at intervals in small amounts and constant stirring (preferably with a wooden spoon). The surface starch meets the boiling broth and together they homogenize creating the creamy consistency that is the hallmark of a well made risotto. Even though the dish is finished with a "mantecato" (a portion of cold butter and grated Parmesan), generally no cream is used. Nowadays one can find all sorts of risottos finished with copious amounts of cream be it the American heavy variety, the French crème fraîche or the Italian mascarpone. These versions, albeit delicious can overshadow what mastering the classic technique offers, a classic creamy dish with no cream.

unkle e's ramblings on risotto!

You want to eat tempura and just about anything fried as soon as possible 'cause they are just tastier that way but the reason behind eating a mushroom or vegetable tempura so quickly is because as your hot cooked vegetables cool down inside the batter they begin to steam, making them less crispy as time goes on. So what do you end up with? Well, soggy tempura, and kulinary katz-n-kittenz, that is never a good thing!

Tempura of Puffball Mushrooms

Serves 8

1 large wild puffball mushroom, wiped clean

1 recipe Tempura Batter, page 175

1–2 quarts soybean oil, for deep-frying, preferably from Michigan

sea salt, to taste

black pepper, freshly ground, to taste

Cut the puffball mushroom into ¼-inch slices like a loaf of bread.

Cut each mushroom slice into 8 wedges like a pizza.

Dip the mushroom wedges into the Tempura Batter and shake off any excess.

Deep-fry the puffballs in a cast iron saucepan or deep fat fryer with the oil at about 375 degrees F. Using tongs carefully turn the mushrooms at intervals to ensure that both sides are cooked equally and then pull them out with a slotted spoon, shaking off any excess oil. Place them on kitchen paper towels to drain and season immediately with the salt and pepper.

Serve immediately.

unkle e's ramblings on puffballs!

I must have been 8 or 10 years old when I saw my second puffball mushroom. I believe it was the summer before when I saw my first. Also called the devil's snuffbox and cream puff, this enormous styrofoam-like globe was nestled onto the forest floor when my buddy ran forward and kicked it. Upon impact the gorgeous globe exploded while a gazillion microscopic spores shot into the air. Coulda been the kewlest thing I had ever seen in my youth. So a year later there I was in the woods alone facing this giant creamy white orb. I streaked across the field, my heart pounding at the thought of my navy blue suede converse all-stars disappearing into the fungal flesh of this mystical mushroom and releasing those way kewl wild spores. I don't remember if I heard the crack first or felt the white hot pain in my ankle searing into my brain when my foot shot into that perfectly symmetrical stone boulder that I mistook for my prized puffball. It took weeks to get over the sprain but I still can't get over the puffball's rich, earthy flavor with that marshmallow like texture.

Chicken Fried Venison Steaks with Beef Jerky Cream Gravy

FOR THE CHICKEN FRIED VENISON STEAKS

Using the textured side of a meat mallet, gently pound each venison steak until well tenderized and uniform in shape about ⅛-inch thick.

In a large non-reactive bowl combine the buttermilk with salt, pepper and hot sauce. Mix to blend and add the venison steaks. The steaks can be marinated up to 24 hours in the buttermilk mixture or used immediately.

In another large bowl combine the rice flour seasoned to taste with the salt and pepper.

Remove the steaks from the buttermilk and shake off any excess. Dredge the steaks in the seasoned rice flour. Shake off the excess flour. For an extra crispy and thick crust repeat the process.

Place the coated steaks on a rack over a sheet tray until ready to fry.

Preheat the oven to 200 degrees F.

Heat ½-inch of the soybean oil in a large, deep cast iron skillet or Dutch oven over medium-high heat until almost smoking.

Fry the steaks in the hot oil until golden brown and cooked through, 1 to 2 minutes per side.

When the steak is done, transfer to a paper-lined tray or plate to drain, and keep warm in the oven. Reserve the cooking skillet with the crumbly bits to make the gravy.

TO MAKE THE BEEF JERKY CREAM GRAVY

Carefully pour out all but ½ cup of the hot oil from the cooking skillet and discard, leaving the crumbly bits on the bottom. Add the flour to the skillet and cook it over medium-high heat, stirring, with the crumbly bits and the reserved oil for 2 to 3 minutes or until the flour is golden brown. Add the chopped red onion, chopped jerky, ¼ cup of the green onions, salt, pepper and hot sauce. Sauté until the vegetables are tender, about 4 to 5 minutes.

Whisk in the Creamline milk little by little, until thoroughly combined and follow with the Roasted Garlic Purée. Cook until the sauce is smooth and thickened, about 8 to 10 minutes.

Serve the venison steaks topped with the Beef Jerky Cream Gravy and garnish with remaining green onions.

Recommended beverage: Brys Estate Merlot

Serves 4

four, 8-ounce venison top round steaks, preferably from Michigan, about ½-inch thick

1½ cups cultured buttermilk

1 teaspoon sea salt

½ teaspoon black pepper, freshly ground, or to taste

Clancy's Fancy Hot Sauce, or similar, to taste

3 cups rice flour

soybean oil, preferably from Michigan, for frying

FOR THE BEEF JERKY CREAM GRAVY

2 tablespoons unbleached all-purpose flour

1 cup red onion, peeled and finely chopped

4 ounces beef jerky, preferably from Michigan, finely chopped

½ cup green onions, finely sliced

1 teaspoon sea salt

1 teaspoon black pepper, freshly ground

Clancy's Fancy Hot Sauce, or similar, to taste

2½ cups Creamline milk (If 2½ cups of Creamline milk is unavailable substitute 2 cups of high quality whole milk combined with ½ a cup of high quality heavy cream.)

2 tablespoons Roasted Garlic Purée, page 88

Cream of Hickory Smoked Tomato Soup

Serves 4–6

5 pounds red or yellow beefsteak tomatoes (cores removed)

sea salt, to taste

black pepper, freshly ground, to taste

Clancy's Fancy Hot Sauce, or similar, to taste

½ cup Roasted Garlic Purée, page 88

2–3 cups heavy cream

Set up your smoker using your choice of hardwoods according to your manufacturers directions.

Place the whole tomatoes core side up on the cooking rack(s) and smoke at 200 degrees F for approximately 1½ to 2 hours or until the tomatoes are smoky, soft and the skin is starting to split. Let the tomatoes cool to room temperature.

When the tomatoes are cool to the touch (they shouldn't be all that hot) gently pull off the tomato skins and discard. Cut the skinless tomatoes into quarters. Place the peeled and quartered tomatoes in a heavy bottomed and non-reactive saucepan along with any of the reserved tomato juice. Roughly break up the soft tomatoes with a large spoon or potato masher.

Begin seasoning with the salt, pepper and hot sauce to taste and continue the seasoning throughout the duration of the preparation. Bring the smoked tomatoes to a boil and add the Roasted Garlic Purée. Reduce the heat to low, and simmer uncovered, stirring frequently and reduce until a very thick purée remains (about 4 to 5 cups). Remove from heat.

Using an immersion blender process the thick smoked tomato purée in the saucepan until smooth or place the smoked tomato mixture in the bowl of a food processor or blender, and purée soup in batches until smooth (If small seeds or bits of skin bother you, the purée may be run through a fine strainer at this point). Return the purée to the pan and stir in the cream until well blended.

Check the seasonings and adjust if necessary. Simmer until heated through, 3 to 5 minutes, taste again and re-season if necessary.

Serve immediately.

Wood Grilled New York Steak Topped with Maytag Blue Cheese Walnut Butter

Preheat your wood burning or gas grill to medium-high heat according to the manufacturers directions.

FOR THE MAYTAG BLUE CHEESE BUTTER

In a medium mixing bowl blend the softened butter and cheese thoroughly and follow with the walnuts. Season the mixture to taste with the sea salt and pepper.

FOR THE STEAKS

Season the steaks to taste with the sea salt and black pepper and the olive oil. Grill the steaks to desired doneness, about 4 minutes per side for medium-rare. Transfer steaks to plates and top each with generous tablespoonful of blue cheese-walnut butter and serve.

Recommended beverage: Renaissance Cellars Cabernet Franc

Serves 4

FOR THE MAYTAG BLUE CHEESE BUTTER

4 ounces unsalted sweet butter, room temperature

4 ounces Maytag Blue cheese, or similar, crumbled

3 tablespoons walnuts, toasted and chopped

sea salt, to taste

black pepper, freshly ground, to taste

FOR THE STEAKS

four 1-inch thick New York steaks, USDA prime grade, or similar, preferably from Michigan

sea salt, to taste

black pepper, freshly ground, to taste

2–3 tablespoons extra virgin cold pressed olive oil

Beef and Pork Pasty with a Classic Suet Crust

Serves 6

FOR THE CRUST

4 cups unbleached all-purpose flour, preferably from Michigan

2 teaspoons sea salt

½ teaspoon baking powder

1½ cups beef suet, ground twice

ice water

FOR THE FILLING

Basic Maple Brine, optional, page 173

1 pound top sirloin, diced and brined

½ pound pork shoulder, diced and brined

2 whole Yukon gold potatoes, peeled and diced

1 large, whole sweet potato, peeled and diced

1 medium, whole rutabaga, peeled and diced

1 large red onion, peeled and diced

1 tablespoon sea salt, or to taste

1 teaspoon black pepper, or to taste

3 tablespoons fresh seasonal herbs, chopped

6 tablespoons Horseradish Butter, page 176

FOR THE BEEF SUET CRUST

In a large bowl, combine flour, salt, baking powder, and suet. Mix well, using your fingers to break down the suet until mixture resembles coarse meal. Pour in enough ice water to gather into a ball. Divide the dough into 6 balls, dust each with flour, and wrap with plastic wrap. Refrigerate for 1 hour.

FOR THE FILLING

Combine the remaining ingredients, except the butter. Roll each ball of dough in a circle on a floured surface to ⅛-inch thickness.

Place 1½ cups filling over half the dough on each circle. Evenly top with the Horseradish Butter. Fold over unfilled side of dough and crimp the edges, sealing by moistening lightly. The pasties should look like half moons.

Preheat the oven to 375 degrees F.

Place the pasties on greased baking sheets and bake for 45 minutes to one hour or until the crust is golden and the pasty is cooked through.

Recommended beverage: Black Star Farms Artisan Red

The pasty like other culinary classics have as many recipes as there are cooks who make them. Some of the additions that add not only taste and texture but also historical significance are dried fruits, the substitution of carrots for the rutabagas and lard, shortening or butter for the beef suet in the crust.

There is some talk of the miners initials made from scraps of dough strategically placed on one end of the pasty so that any leftovers can be traced back to the proper miner.

Pasties are served with an assortment of toppings—choose your favorite: glaze of melted butter, beef or poultry gravy or ketchup.

Makes about 6½ pounds of scrapple or about 2, 9x5 loaf pans. The scrapple can be easily frozen but it's best to freeze the scrapple in slices that allows you to prepare a hot scrapple dish in minutes from the freezer

Scrapple

Makes 2 loaves

6 pounds pork ribs, country style

1 large ham hock, smoked

1 large white onion, peeled and quartered

1 large carrot, peeled and quartered

2 large celery ribs, quartered

2 large bay leaves

4 quarts water, approximately

sea salt, to taste

black pepper, freshly ground, to taste

1½ teaspoons dried thyme

2 teaspoons rubbed sage

1 teaspoon ground savory

⅛ teaspoon allspice, or to taste

⅛ teaspoon nutmeg, or to taste

⅛ teaspoon cloves, or to taste

3 cups cornmeal, preferably from Michigan, yellow or white

¼ cup Roasted Garlic Purée, page 88

fresh pork lard, butter, or oil, 1 teaspoon per slice

unbleached all-purpose flour, for dusting, preferably from Michigan

TO MAKE THE SCRAPPLE

The day before you plan to make the scrapple place the fresh pork ribs, smoked ham hock, onions, carrots, celery, bay leaves and water in an 8-quart stockpot. Add salt and pepper. Slowly bring to a boil; reduce heat, cover and simmer until pork is tender, about 2 hours. Carefully remove the meat and strain the pork broth (discarding the vegetables).

Refrigerate both the meat and strained broth. When the meat is cool enough to handle, remove the bones and discard with the excess fat and skin. Chop the meat finely and set aside. When the broth is cool enough remove the fat from the top and reserve broth.

Place 2½ quarts of the reserved and defatted broth in a 5-quart pot. Add the thyme, sage, savory, allspice, nutmeg and cloves. Bring to a boil and gradually add the corn-meal and Roasted Garlic Purée, stirring or whisking rapidly until it is all combined. Reduce the heat to medium or medium-low and continue to cook, stirring often, until the mixture is very thick, about 15 minutes. If it gets too thick, just add a little more of the reserved broth and stir well.

Add the meat and blend well to combine. Reduce the heat to low and cook for an additional 15 minutes, stirring occasionally. After a couple minutes, taste for seasoning and adjust as desired. At this stage it is important that the scrapple be extremely well seasoned or the flavor will suffer when fried.

Butter two 9x5 loaf pans or similar. Pour half the mixture into each pan. Cover with foil and refrigerate overnight or until chilled and solid.

Remove the loaf from the pan and place on cutting surface. Slice into about ¼ to ½-inch slices. Dust each slice lightly in the flour while heating a heavy bottomed skillet over medium-high heat. Add a teaspoon of lard, butter or oil to the pan per slice. When the pan is hot and the fat is sizzling add the scrapple slices. It is critical with scrapple to let each side brown thoroughly before attempting to turn it over or it's possible that it can stick and fall apart. Cook both sides until golden brown and crispy and the center is warmed through.

Serve as is or as part of a hearty breakfast drizzled with Michigan maple syrup paired with eggs and fruit. If you would rather follow in the footsteps of the Pennsylvania Dutch, sauce the crispy scrapple with a bit of ketchup or apple butter!

Maple Chocolate Truffles

In a medium, heavy bottomed non-reactive saucepan over medium-high heat bring the cream just to a simmer, making sure it doesn't boil over. Pour the hot cream over the chopped chocolate in a heatproof bowl and let stand about 10 minutes to melt the chocolate.

Add the vanilla and maple sugar, stir until smooth. Set aside to cool for 1 hour at room temperature.

In the bowl of a mixer fitted with the paddle attachment beat the chocolate at medium speed until it gets thick and light colored, about 4 to 5 minutes. Spread over the bottom of a baking dish and smooth the top and press plastic wrap against the surface.

Refrigerate about 2 hours, or until firm.

Place the cocoa powder in a deep plate or shallow bowl. Use a melon ball scooper or tablespoon to scoop out balls of chocolate about the size of a walnut; set them on the plate with the cocoa powder and roll using 2 forks to completely coat with the cocoa powder. Then use the forks to carefully transfer them to a parchment lined baking sheet.

Can be refrigerated up to 2 weeks.

Recommended beverage: Black Star Farms Sirius Pear Dessert Wine

Makes about 2 dozen

1 cup heavy cream

1 pound bittersweet chocolate, chopped

2 teaspoons vanilla extract, pure

2–4 tablespoons maple sugar, preferably from Michigan

1 cup cocoa powder, unsweetened, for dusting

Crispy Hot Maple Chocolate Truffles

Makes about 2 dozen

1 recipe Maple Chocolate Truffles, page 169

2 cups rice flour

3 whole eggs, beaten with a bit of salt

1½ cups fresh breadcrumbs, ground fine

1½ cups beet sugar, preferably from Michigan, or similar

¼ cup Saigon cinnamon, or similar

soybean oil, preferably from Michigan, for frying

Prepare the chocolate truffles as in the Maple Chocolate Truffle recipe (page 169) but disregard the final rolling in cocoa powder. After scooping the balls of chocolate place immediately onto the prepared baking sheet. Place the baking sheet into a freezer for 2 to 3 hours or until the truffle is frozen solid. It is crucial that the truffles are frozen for the frying.

Set up a breading station with plates of the flour, the beaten eggs, and the fresh breadcrumbs mixed with the sugar and cinnamon.

Roll 2 to 4 frozen truffles at a time first in the flour. Roll the flour-coated truffle in the palms of your hands packing the flour around the truffle. Place into the beaten eggs and completely coat. Remove from the eggs and let the excess drip off and place immediately into the breadcrumbs. Coat thoroughly in the crumbs and as with the flour procedure, roll the crumb-coated truffle quickly in your hands pressing the breadcrumbs into the truffle. Repeat the entire procedure with the same truffle for a second coating and place on a prepared cookie sheet. Repeat with the remaining truffles. When all the truffles are double coated place the cookie sheet into the freezer for 2 to 3 hours or until frozen solid. All of this can be done up to a week in advance.

Preheat the soybean oil to 375 degrees F.

Working in small batches so as not to crowd the oil, fry the truffles for 10 to 15 seconds or until a strong crust has formed and immediately remove and drain on paper towels and serve immediately.

Recommended beverage: Leelanau Muscat

STEAMER FARRELL, FLAGSHIP OF THE PITTSBURGH S. S. CO., LOCKING DOWN IN THE SABIN LOCK

Great Lakes Pantry

Fish Stock

Makes 3 quarts

5 pounds whitefish carcasses, skin and fins removed

2 tablespoons extra virgin cold pressed olive oil

1 whole white onion, peeled and thinly sliced

12 ounces button mushrooms, thinly sliced

2 stalks celery, thinly sliced

12 cloves fresh hardnecked garlic, separated, peeled and smashed

3 whole bay leaves

4 sprigs parsley

1 cup dry white wine

3 quarts water

Cut the fish carcasses in manageable pieces and rinse well in several changes of water to remove any blood.

Heat the olive oil over high heat in large stockpot. Add the onions, mushrooms, celery, garlic, bay leaves, and parsley. Reduce the heat down to medium and cook for 4 to 5 minutes.

Add the white wine, fish carcasses and top off with the water. Bring the mixture to a simmer and skim off and discard the white froth as it rises to the surface. Maintain a gentle simmer for about 30 minutes. Remove the broth from the heat and strain it through a fine sieve and discard all the remaining solids.

The stock can be refrigerated 3 or 4 days or can be frozen up to 6 months.

To make into a glace, place the broth or stock into a large stockpot over high heat and reduce until a cup to ½ cup of thick syrup remains. Can be frozen and used for other recipes. Be aware that heavily reduced fish stocks tend to be extremely strong and bitter. Use sparingly.

Mushroom Broth

Makes about 2 cups

2 tablespoons extra virgin cold pressed olive oil

1 pound button mushrooms, quartered

2 shallots, peeled and sliced

1 whole fresh hardnecked garlic head, split across the equator

2 tablespoons flat leaf parsley, chopped

4 sprigs fresh thyme

3 cups water (just enough to cover)

sea salt, to taste

black pepper, freshly ground, to taste

In a large, heavy bottomed non-reactive saucepan heat the olive oil over medium-high heat until sizzling. Add the mushrooms and cook until the mushrooms are a deep brown and have caramelized about 15 to 20 minutes. Resist the urge to shake the pan or stir the mushrooms too much, the more the mushrooms move about the pan the harder it will be for them to caramelize.

Add the shallots, garlic, parsley and thyme to the mushrooms and cover with the water. Stir well, scraping up any brown bits stuck on the bottom of the pan and season to taste with the salt and pepper.

Bring to a boil over medium-high heat for 1 to 2 minutes then turn down the heat to a very low simmer and let cook for about 30 to 45 minutes.

Strain the broth through a fine mesh strainer pressing hard on the mushrooms and vegetables to extract as much flavor as possible.

Broth can be refrigerated 3 or 4 days or can be frozen up to 6 months.

B rine meats, poultry and shellfish before cooking or smoking. Use the following times for guidelines:

→ whole chicken, 24 hours
→ whole turkey, 24 hours
→ whole bone in raw pork loin, 24 hours
→ whole pork tenderloin, 6 hours
→ shrimp, shelled and butterflied, 1 hour
→ fish fillets, 1 hour

Basic Maple Brine

Bring the quart of water to a boil in a medium saucepan and add the salt, sugar, lime juice, hot sauce, bay leaves and garlic. Remove from the heat and stir until the salt and sugar are dissolved. Let cool to room temperature.

In a suitable bowl or food safe bucket add the cooled brine and top off with the ice water and stir to blend.

The brine is now ready to use.

Makes 4 quarts

1 quart water

½ cup sea salt

½ cup maple sugar, preferably from Michigan

¼ cup fresh lime juice, and the squeezed lime halves

3 tablespoons Clancy's Fancy Hot Sauce, or similar

6 bay leaves, broken

12 cloves fresh hardnecked garlic, crushed

3 quarts water, iced

Shrimp Stock

In a large, heavy bottomed non-reactive stockpot heat the olive oil over medium-high heat. Add onion, fennel, carrot and garlic. Sauté 5 minutes.

Add the raw shrimp shells (and heads if available) and sauté until the shells turn bright pink, about 5 minutes.

Add the white wine, tomatoes, and boil until almost all of the wine evaporates, about 5 minutes.

Add the water, peppercorns, thyme, parsley and bay leaf.

Bring to a boil. Reduce heat and simmer for about 30 minutes.

Carefully strain the stock; discard the solids. Stock may be refrigerated 3 or 4 days or can be frozen up to 6 months.

For a darker richer stock roast the shrimp shells in a preheated 425 degree F oven for 10 to 20 minutes or until the shells are just charred and continue with recipe.

If more stock is needed, bottled clam juice or a low sodium light chicken broth can be used as an extender.

Makes about 3 quarts

2 tablespoons extra virgin cold pressed olive oil

1 medium red onion, peeled and chopped

1 medium fennel bulb, chopped

1 medium carrot, chopped

6 cloves fresh hardnecked garlic, crushed

2 ½ pounds shrimp shells, including heads if you can get them!

¼ cup dry white wine, preferably from Michigan

1 cup tomatoes, chopped

3 quarts water

10 black peppercorns, whole

6 fresh thyme sprigs

6 fresh parsley sprigs

1 bay leaf

Maple Smoked Jalapeño and Lime Glaze

Makes about ¾ cup

½ cup maple syrup, preferably from Michigan

2 large Hickory Smoked Jalapeños, ribbed and seeded, page 184

¼ cup lime juice

1 tablespoon Roasted Garlic Purée, page 88

sea salt, to taste

Combine all the ingredients in the bowl of a small food processor or blender. Process until smooth. Taste and adjust seasonings as necessary. If the glaze is too thin add more lime juice or water to taste.

Can be refrigerated up to 2 weeks.

Kahlúa Sour Cream

Makes about 1 cup

1 cup sour cream, preferably from Michigan

1/4 cup powdered sugar, or to taste

12 tablespoons Kahlúa, or similar, or to taste

In a medium mixing bowl blend together the sour cream, powdered sugar and Kahlúa. Refrigerate until needed.

> If powdered sugar is unavailable regular sugar can be substituted. The great thing about powdered sugar in a recipe like this is that it "melts" instantly into the recipe without heat. Regular sugar works well but requires a bit more time to "melt" because of the coarse grind. If you do use a regular sugar give yourself about 30 minutes or an hour to achieve the same creamy result.

Roasted Chestnuts

Makes 2 pounds

2 pounds whole Michigan chestnuts, or similar

Preheat the oven to 400 degrees F.

Use a small, sharp, paring knife to make an "X" fashioned slash (½ to 1-inch) on the flat side of each chestnut.

Arrange slashed nuts in a single layer on a baking sheet and bake for 10 minutes.

Peel with a small sharp knife and eat directly from the shell.

Chowder Crackers

Preheat oven to 425 degrees F.

Combine all dry ingredients in food processor. Add butter and pulse quickly, until it looks like "coarse meal". Add the milk and process 3 seconds. Remove to floured surface, knead 10 seconds and chill the dough.

Roll out the dough ⅛-inch thick and cut in any desired shape using cookie cutters. Place the crackers on a prepared cookie sheet and gently brush the tops with a bit of the milk and top each cracker with a sprinkle of the coarse sea salt.

Bake the crackers in the center of the preheated oven for 5 to 7 minutes or until light brown.

Makes about 2 dozen small crackers

2 cups unbleached all-purpose flour

1 tablespoon baking powder

1 teaspoon sea salt

4 ounces unsalted sweet butter, chilled and cubed

4 ounces whole milk

FOR GARNISH

1 ounce whole milk

2 tablespoons coarse sea salt

Tempura Batter

Mix all the dry ingredients in a mixing bowl and slowly add the beer, lemon juice and zest. Mix until smooth, and then season with the hot sauce. Use immediately.

Makes; about 1½ cups

1 cup rice flour

2 tablespoons yellow cornmeal, preferably from Michigan

2 teaspoons sea salt

1 cup artisan lager, preferably from Michigan

2 teaspoons fresh lemon juice

1 tablespoon fresh lemon zest

3 shots Clancy's Fancy Hot Sauce, or similar

Horseradish Butter

Makes about 1½ pounds

1 pound unsalted sweet butter, softened

6–8 ounces prepared horseradish, drained

black pepper, freshly ground, to taste

sea salt, to taste

Cream the butter in a mixer at medium speed. Add the drained horseradish and blend until fully incorporated. Roll the butter in plastic wrap and chill until firm.

Use as a topping for hot foods, a "stuffing" for fish or poultry, or a last minute enrichment for soups or sauces.

Maytag Blue Cheese Cream

Makes about 1½ cups

¼ pound Maytag Blue cheese, or similar, crumbled

1 ¼ cups sour cream, preferably from Michigan

2 tablespoons white wine vinegar

1 teaspoon red wine vinegar

1 teaspoon Worcestershire sauce

¼ teaspoon Roasted Garlic Purée, page 88

½ teaspoon sea salt

½ teaspoon black pepper, freshly ground, or to taste

¼ teaspoon Clancy's Fancy Hot Sauce, or similar

In a medium bowl using a rubber spatula, mix the Maytag Blue cheese with the sour cream until well blended. Add the remaining ingredients, stir to combine and serve.

CASTLE ROCK, ST. IGNACE

Sun Dried Tomato Pesto

Combine the tomatoes, Roasted Garlic Purée, lemon juice, olive oil, oregano, basil and salt in a blender or food processor.

Process until the mixture is a bit coarse but homogenous.

Can be refrigerated up to 1 month.

Makes about 2 cups

1½ pounds sun dried tomatoes packed in oil, drained

½ teaspoon Roasted Garlic Purée, page 88

1 tablespoon fresh lemon juice

2 teaspoons extra virgin cold pressed olive oil

½ teaspoon fresh oregano, chopped

7 leaves fresh basil, chopped

sea salt, to taste

Leelanau Red Wine and Vanilla Syrup

In a large, non-reactive heavy bottomed saucepan over medium-high heat place the wine, beet sugar and vanilla extract. Reduce the mixture by 75 percent or until it's thick and syrupy. Let cool. Can be refrigerated up to 1 month.

Makes about 1 pint

2 quarts Leelanau red table wine, or similar

½ cup beet sugar, preferably from Michigan, or similar

1 teaspoon pure vanilla extract

Red Onion and Walnut Vinaigrette

In a large bowl mix the red onions, vinegar, mustard, salt, pepper and hot sauce to taste.

Let sit for at least one hour.

Whisk in the oil to create a creamy emulsion.

Can be refrigerated for several weeks. Whisk again at serving time to create a thick emulsion.

Makes 1½ cups

½ cup red onions, peeled and cut julienne

½ cup sherry wine vinegar

1 tablespoon Dijon mustard

sea salt, to taste

black pepper, freshly ground, to taste

Clancy's Fancy Hot Sauce, or similar, to taste

1 cup walnut oil

Compound Butter

Makes about 1 pound

1 pound unsalted butter, softened

1 cup herbs*, tightly packed and freshly chopped

¼ cup lemon or lime juice

sea salt (optional)

Cream the butter in a mixer at medium speed.

Add the herbs, lemon or lime juice and mix until totally incorporated.

Roll the butter in plastic wrap and chill until firm.

The compound butter can be frozen up to six months well wrapped.

*Any herb you like can be used, just make sure it is fresh and in good shape. Don't limit yourself to just herbs; black truffles, crab, roasted garlic, maple syrup, dried fruit and cheese can be used and even in combinations. You are limited only by your imagination.

TRUFFLE BUTTER

For black truffle butter use 6–8 ounces (or to taste) of chopped whole black truffles or chopped black truffle peelings per pound of butter.

LIME BUTTER

For a fresh lime or lemon butter use 6–8 ounces (or to taste) of fresh lemon or lime juice per pound of butter.

✦ Use as a topping for hot foods, a "stuffing" for fish or poultry, or a last minute enrichment for soups or sauces.

Maple Salt

Makes about 1½ cups

2–3 tablespoons maple sugar, preferably from Michigan

1 cup sea salt

¼ cup black pepper, freshly ground, or to taste

1 tablespoon aji amarillo, coarsely ground

Combine all the ingredients in a bowl and stir or whisk to mix well.

Store the salt in a sealed container preferably away from heat and light in a cool dark pantry or freezer. The blend will keep for several months.

Herb Vinaigrette

Combine the vinegar, shallots, Roasted Garlic Purée, herbs, salt, pepper and the optional hot sauce in a bowl.

Let sit for at least one hour for flavors to meld.

Slowly whisk in the oil and continue whisking until thoroughly emulsified.

Store, refrigerated, in an airtight container, will keep for 3 days.

Whisk to combine before serving.

Makes about 1 cup

¼ cup champagne vinegar

2 tablespoons shallots, peeled and minced

1 tablespoon Roasted Garlic Purée, page 88

¼ cup assorted seasonal fresh herbs, chopped

1 teaspoon sea salt, or to taste

black pepper, freshly ground, to taste

Clancy's Fancy Hot Sauce, or similar, optional

¾ cup extra virgin cold pressed olive oil

unkle e's ramblings on vinaigrettes!

Show me a well made balanced vinaigrette and you will find someone who truly 'gets' what cooking is all about—even though vinaigrette at its most basic has only three components: acid, oil and flavorings.

In the case of a classically prepared French vinaigrette the acid in question is vinegar. But that doesn't mean that all French styles of dressings need to have vinegar. Citronette is a dressing or vinaigrette if you will, that uses lemon juice or "citron" as the acid. You the chef, my friends can use any culinary acid your little heart desires.

Oil is the necessary lubricant that spreads out the acid flavor. A tablespoon of white wine vinegar might be a bit too much for your palette but once you add twice the amount of oil in, let's say a fruity extra virgin olive oil and the puckery vinegar will be tempered with the luscious oil. Like the choice of acids, the choice of oils is even bigger—olive, walnut, avocado, soybean, canola, the list goes on.

Flavorings can be as simple as a good quality sea salt and pepper to whatever the season offers. Mixed fresh herbs, a dice of heirloom tomatoes, and wild mushrooms are just a few options.

Thyme Lime Honey

Makes about 1 cup

1 cup clover honey, preferably from Michigan

2 tablespoons unsalted sweet butter

2 whole limes, juiced

1 tablespoon fresh thyme leaves, chopped

In a small non-reactive saucepan heat up the honey, butter, lime juice and fresh thyme over medium heat until well blended and hot. Use immediately.

Feel free to substitute any fresh seasonal herb to compliment the honey and coordinate with whatever you may be serving the honey with.

Cranberry Syrup

Makes ¼ cup

4 cups cranberry juice, your favorite brand with sugar added

In a non-reactive medium saucepan reduce the cranberry juice to a syrup, around ¼ of a cup.

Can be refrigerated up to 1 month.

Parsley Oil

Makes about 2½ cups

2 bunches flat leaf parsley, cleaned

¼ cup Roasted Garlic Purée, page 88

sea salt, to taste

Clancy's Fancy Hot Sauce, to taste

2 cups extra virgin cold pressed olive oil

Assemble the masticating juicer, or similar, according to the manufacturers directions.

Dip an appropriate amount of parsley in water briefly and shake to remove excess water leaving just what's clinging to the stems and leaves.

Pass the parsley through the running machine.

Add a slight amount of water to the discarded pulp and rerun through the machine to completely extract all of the juice.

Place the parsley juice, Roasted Garlic Purée, salt and hot sauce in the bowl of a food processor or blender and drizzle in the oil with the machine running until a rich purée is obtained.

Store refrigerated in an airtight container for 3 to 4 weeks.

Apple Pâte Brisée

Mix the flour, butter, and salt together very lightly, so that the pieces of butter remain visible throughout the flour.

Add the ice-cold cider and mix very fast with your hand just enough that the dough masses. Cut the dough in half. The pieces of butter should still be visible. It's best to allow the dough to rest chilled for 1 or 2 hours, but can be used right away.

Wrapped properly, it can be kept in the refrigerator for 2 or 3 days, or it can be frozen.

Makes enough for 2 galettes

3 cups unbleached all-purpose flour, preferably from Michigan

½ pound unsalted sweet butter, cold, and cut into thin slices or coarse shavings

½ teaspoon sea salt

¾ cup fresh apple cider, preferably from Michigan and unpasteurized

Profiteroles

Heat the milk, butter, and sea salt over medium heat until scalded. When the butter is melted, add the flour all at once and beat it with a wooden spoon until the mixture masses together and forms dough. Cook, stirring constantly, over low heat for 2 minutes. The flour will begin to coat the bottom of the pan and mass into a ball.

Quickly dump the dough mixture (careful it's very hot) into the bowl of a stand mixer fitted with the whisk attachment. Add the eggs one by one and mix in each one thoroughly before adding the others. Depending on the age of your flour and the length of time it takes to "mass" the dough, you might not need all of the eggs or you could even need more. You are looking for a tight, thick dough that just falls off the spoon.

Quickly and carefully (it's hot) spoon the mixture into a pastry bag fitted with a large star or plain round tip. Pipe in mounds, 1 ½-inches wide and 1-inch high onto a baking sheet lined with parchment paper. You should have approximately 16 to 18 puffs.

Bake for 20 minutes, or until lightly browned, then turn off the oven and allow them to sit for another 10 minutes, until they sound hollow when tapped on the bottom. Make a small slit in the side of each puff to allow the steam to escape.

Set aside to cool, use as needed.

Makes 16–18 puffs

1 cup Creamline milk, preferably from Michigan (I prefer to use a Creamline or non-homogenized whole organic milk. If this particular style of milk is unavailable use the best quality whole milk you can find and add ½ cup heavy cream)

¼ pound unsalted sweet butter

1 pinch sea salt

1 cup unbleached all-purpose flour, preferably from Michigan

4 extra large eggs, preferably from Michigan

Hickory Smoked Tomatoes

Makes about 4½ pounds

5 pounds beefsteak tomatoes, cored

Set up your smoker with hickory according to your manufacturers directions.

Place the whole tomatoes core side up on the cooking rack(s) and smoke at 250 degrees F for approximately 1 ½ to 2 hours or until the tomatoes are smoky, soft and the skin is starting to split. Let the tomatoes cool to room temperature.

The tomatoes can be used as is or stored in the refrigerator well wrapped for 3 to 5 days.

Hickory Smoked Tomato Vinaigrette

Makes about 1¾ cups

1 cup Hickory Smoked Tomato Salsa, page 87

1 teaspoon Dijon mustard

¼ cup French white wine vinegar

sea salt, to taste

black pepper, freshly ground, to taste

Clancy's Fancy Hot Sauce, to taste

½ cup extra virgin cold pressed olive oil

In a large non-reactive bowl mix the Hickory Smoked Tomato Salsa, mustard, vinegar, salt, pepper and hot sauce to taste. Let sit for at least one hour. Whisk in the oil to create a creamy emulsion.

Can be refrigerated for several weeks. Whisk again at serving time to create a thick emulsion.

Roasted Tomato Sauce

Preheat your oven to 375 degrees F.

In a large mixing bowl add the tomatoes, onions, garlic, bay leaves and herbs. Season with the salt, pepper, and olive oil; toss to mix. Pour the tomato mixture into a roasting pan and pour in the vegetable broth.

Place in the center of the preheated oven and cook until the skins are charred and the sauce begins to thicken, about an hour.

At this point the "sauce" can be used as is or for a more traditional style, pulse in a food processor or blender for a smooth consistency.

—€ The beauty of this sauce is using whatever herbs happen to be seasonally available. In the heat of the summer big green leaves of basil would be traditional and perfect for summer. Later in the fall some woodsy sage or rosemary would give your sauce a stronger heartier personality.

Makes about 3 cups

3 pounds Roma tomatoes, cored and split stem to core

1 large red onion, peeled and cut julienne

½ cup hardnecked garlic cloves, peeled, or similar

6 bay leaves

1 ½ cups fresh seasonal herbs, chopped

sea salt, to taste

black pepper, freshly ground, to taste

½ cup extra virgin cold pressed olive oil

½ cup vegetable broth

Whole Egg Mayonnaise

In a blender or food processor, combine the eggs, Dijon, Roasted Garlic Purée, vinegar, salt and the hot sauce. Blend at lowest speed to combine.

With blender still running increase the speed to high and add the soybean oil in a slow, steady stream until it is incorporated and thick. Follow with the olive oil and let the machine run another minute to completely blend the mixture.

Serve immediately, or refrigerate, covered, for up to 2 days.

—€ Wanna spice up your mayonnaise? Howabouta hickory smoked jalapeño version?

—€ Clean two or three good sized hickory smoked jalapeños and remove the ribs and the seeds. Finely dice the flesh and mix with 2 cups of the Whole Egg Mayonnaise and refrigerate for 1 hour for the flavors to develop.

Makes about 2 cups

2 whole large eggs, preferably from Michigan

2 tablespoons Dijon mustard

1 tablespoon Roasted Garlic Purée, page 88

3 tablespoons white wine vinegar

sea salt, to taste

Clancy's Fancy Hot Sauce, to taste

1 ½ cups soybean oil, preferably from Michigan

¼ cup extra virgin cold pressed olive oil

Hickory Smoked Jalapeños

Makes 12 jalapeños

12 medium whole jalapeños

Set up your smoker with hickory according to your manufacturers directions.

Place the whole jalapeños on the cooking rack and smoke at 250 degrees F for approximately 1 ½ to 2 hours or until the jalapeños are smoky, soft and the skin is starting to split. Let the jalapeños cool to room temperature.

The jalapeños can be used as is or stored in the refrigerator well wrapped for 3 to 5 days.

Hickory Smoked Jalapeño Cream

Makes about 1 cup

1–2 large Hickory Smoked Jalapeños, recipe above

2–3 tablespoons fresh lime juice

1 cup sour cream

sea salt, to taste

Wearing rubber gloves, stem, seed, rib and finely dice the smoked jalapeños. Place in a mixing bowl with the sour cream, lime juice and salt. Stir to combine thoroughly.

Serve immediately, or refrigerate, covered, for up to 5 days.

> Why one or two jalapeños? Well katz-n-kittenz how hot do you want it!? Obviously the more jalapeño the more heat. Also remember that quite a bit of firepower is stored in the ribs and seeds of the jalapeño so if you want something really smoking—leave 'em in!

Raspberry Sauce

Makes about 1 cup

2 cups raspberries, fresh or frozen (if frozen thaw first)

lemon juice, fresh, to taste

12 tablespoons powdered sugar, or to taste

Purée raspberries, lemon juice and powdered sugar in a blender until smooth. Strain the raspberry purée and discard the seeds. Refrigerate until needed.

It seems that every batch of raspberries are different so the sugar and the lemon juice should be added to your own personal taste.

Coffee Maple Glaze

In a medium, heavy bottomed non-reactive saucepan over medium heat add 1 tablespoon of the butter and follow with the shallots. After 3 to 5 minutes the shallots should be soft and translucent. Add the beet sugar, aji amarillo powder, vinegar, red wine, and maple syrup.

Turn the heat down to medium-low, and let simmer until the mixture begins to reduce and achieves a light syrup-like consistency. Add the espresso and simmer for five more minutes.

When the mixture is thick whisk in the remaining butter and strain.

Serve warm over the Grilled New York Strip Steak or try it on roast chicken or pork.

Serves 4

1 tablespoon unsalted sweet butter, plus 2 tablespoons

3 tablespoons shallots, peeled and minced

3 tablespoons beet sugar, preferably from Michigan, or similar

1 teaspoon aji amarillo powder, or similar

½ cup red wine vinegar

½ cup red wine, dry, preferably from Michigan

3 tablespoons maple syrup, preferably from Michigan

3 ounces espresso, brewed

Basil Walnut Pesto

Prepare an ice water bath in a large bowl, and bring a large pot of water to a boil. Put the basil in a large sieve and blanch the herb by plunging it into the boiling water. Cook for about 15 seconds. Remove, shake off the excess water, then plunge the basil immediately into the ice water bath stirring quickly so it cools as fast as possible. Drain well.

Squeeze the water out of the basil with your hands until very dry. Roughly chop the basil and put in a bar blender or smaller food processor. Add the Roasted Garlic Purée, salt and pepper to taste, olive oil, walnuts, and the optional vitamin C powder. Blend for at least 30 seconds then add the cheese and pulse to combine.

The pesto will keep several days in a tightly sealed container in the refrigerator. When ready to use, add the lime juice to brighten the flavor.

Makes about ¾ of a cup

2 cups fresh basil leaves, firmly packed

1 tablespoon Roasted Garlic Purée, page 88

sea salt, to taste

black pepper, freshly ground, to taste

⅓ cup extra virgin cold pressed olive oil

3 tablespoons walnuts, toasted

⅛ teaspoon vitamin C, powdered, optional

¼ cup Wisantigo Parmesan for serving

¼ cup lime juice, freshly squeezed

Beet Sugar Simple Syrup

Makes about 2¼ cups

2 cups beet sugar, preferably from Michigan, or similar

pinch sea salt

2 cups water

In a medium, heavy bottomed non-reactive saucepan over medium heat add the sugar, salt and water.

Simmer for 2 minutes stirring until the sugar has dissolved. Remove from the heat and let cool to room temperature.

Can be refrigerated up to 1 month.

It is said that sugar beets were first grown in Michigan in 1839 on an experimental basis. In the early 1900s there were as many as 25 processing factories in Michigan. Today, there is just one sugar company operating in Michigan, Michigan Sugar Company—but it's a biggie! Michigan Sugar is the largest beet sugar processor east of the Mississippi River and fourth largest in the United States.

Headquartered in Bay City it has approximately 1,300 grower-owners, employing 1,700 seasonal employees and 450 year-round employees. It has four operating factories in Bay City, Caro, Croswell and Sebewaing, and three warehouse terminals located in Michigan and Ohio. It generates nearly $300 million in direct economic activity annually in the local communities in which it operates. Its combined factories have a beet slicing capacity of 22,000 tons per day and an ability to produce about one billion pounds of sugar each year, which it markets under the Pioneer and Big Chief brand names. In 2003, our Michigan farmers harvested 178,000 acres of sugar beets grown in 16 counties in Michigan's Saginaw Valley, Thumb, Central, and South Eastern area. So when you gastronauts are performing your weekly shopping you're grabbing Michigan beet sugar—aren't cha?!?!

Lemon Vinaigrette

Combine the lemon and orange juices with shallots, salt and pepper in a suitable bowl and let sit for at least one hour for the shallots to soften and the flavors to combine.

Whisk in the olive oil in a slow stream to combine.

Taste and adjust seasonings.

Can be refrigerated for several weeks. Whisk again at serving time to create a thick emulsion.

Makes about 2 cups

2 whole lemons, squeezed

½ orange, squeezed

1 shallot, peeled and finely chopped

1 teaspoon sea salt

½ teaspoon black pepper, freshly ground, or to taste

1½ cups extra virgin cold pressed olive oil

Roasted Garlic Mashed Potatoes

Cut the washed Yukon Gold potatoes into quarters, place in a large stock pot with the salt and cover with cold water. Bring to a boil, then simmer until the potatoes are fork tender about 20 to 30 minutes.

Drain well in a colander. While the potatoes are still warm, press them through a potato ricer or food mill and into a mixing bowl. Add the Roasted Garlic Purée and softened butter and using a wooden spoon gently whip the potatoes to blend. Add the heavy cream in a slow stream using some or all of the cream until you achieve your preferred consistency.

Season with the salt, pepper and hot sauce and blend. Taste the potatoes and adjust the seasonings if necessary.

Use immediately.

Serves 6–8

2½ pounds Yukon Gold potatoes, preferably from Michigan

1 tablespoon sea salt

¼ cup Roasted Garlic Purée, page 88

6 ounces unsalted sweet butter, softened

¾–1 cup heavy cream, warmed

sea salt, to taste

black pepper, freshly ground, to taste

Clancy's Fancy Hot Sauce, or similar, to taste

Lake Effect is an all-purpose seasoning blend that heightens the flavors of seafood, poultry, meats and vegetables with the punch of Bolivian aji amarillo peppers that finishes with the sweet caress of Michigan maple sugar.

The ají pepper, is a unique species of chili pepper with several different breeds. The most common are simply differentiated by color, like "yellow hot pepper" or ají amarillo. These peppers have a distinctive, fruity flavor, and are commonly ground into colorful powders for use in cooking, each identified by its color. Always a staple in my home growing up, I love the opportunity to blend my ancestral roots with my Michigan kitchen.

Lake Effect Seasoning

Makes about ¾ cup

2 tablespoons sea salt

1 tablespoon maple sugar, preferably from Michigan

2 ½ tablespoons smoked paprika

2 tablespoons roasted garlic powder

1 tablespoon black pepper, freshly ground, or to taste

1 tablespoon onion powder

1 tablespoon aji amarillo powder, or cayenne

1 tablespoon dried oregano

1 tablespoon dried thyme

Can be scaled up or down as needed.

Combine all the ingredients in a mixing bowl and blend well.

Store the rub in a sealed container preferably away from heat and light in a cool, dark pantry or freezer. The blend will keep for several months.

Cornmeal Porridge

Serves 3–6

1½ cups chicken broth, freshly made or high quality boxed

1½ cups heavy cream

½ teaspoon nutmeg, freshly grated

¾ teaspoon sea salt

1 dash Clancy's Fancy Hot Sauce, or similar

2 tablespoons Roasted Garlic Purée, page 88

5 tablespoons cornmeal, preferably from Michigan

5 tablespoons semolina

¼ cup fresh cow's milk mozzarella, grated

¼ cup Wisantigo Parmesan, or similar, grated

Combine the stock and cream in a heavy bottomed saucepan and bring to a simmer. Add the nutmeg, salt, hot sauce and Roasted Garlic Purée.

Whisk in the cornmeal and semolina and cook over very low heat, whisking regularly, until the grains are soft, about 8 minutes. Whisk in the cheeses.

Use immediately.

Porridge is a ratio of dry to wet ingredients rather than a recipe. For firm porridge, it's one to three. For soft porridge, the ratio of dry to wet is one to five or six.

Demi-Glace

FOR THE BONES AND VEGETABLES

Preheat the oven to 475 degrees F.

Drizzle half the soybean oil into a heavy bottomed roasting pan large enough to hold the veal bones in a single layer. Place the bones into the pan and roast for about 45 minutes to one hour.

In a large mixing bowl add the chopped carrots, onions, garlic, celery and leeks. Drizzle with the remaining oil and toss thoroughly.

After about 45 minutes check the bones. Once they have started to brown and cara-melize, turn them over and smear the bones with tomato paste and mix in the chopped vegetables.

Return the pan to the oven, stir bones and vegetables every 15 minutes for another 45 minutes to one hour or until the bones and vegetables are nicely browned and caramelized.

FOR THE STOCK

Using tongs or a large spoon place the roasted bones and vegetables into a 10 to 12 quart stockpot. Pour off the excess fat from the roasting pan and discard.

Place the roasting pan onto the stovetop and over medium heat add the red wine and deglaze by scraping the bottom with a wooden spoon to loosen up the kulinary kibbles-n-bits.

Pour the contents of the roasting pan into the stockpot adding the peppercorns, thyme and bay leaves with just enough cold water to cover by 2 to 3 inches.

Bring the stock to a quick boil over medium-high heat, then immediately turn the heat to low. While the stock simmers, skim the fat and foam off the top a few times, as needed. After approximately 8 hours the stock should be reduced by almost half and you should end up with about 3 to 3 1/2 quarts of liquid.

Using a slotted spoon lift out the bones and vegetables and discard. Strain the reduced liquid through a fine strainer into a clean pot. Skim any fat from the stock, either with a ladle or by placing it into the refrigerator and remove the fat once it has solidified.

FOR THE DEMI-GLACE

Bring the veal stock up to a boil and then reduce the heat to a simmer, over medium to medium-high heat for about another two hours or until reduced by half. Once it has reduced by half, it should be quite a bit darker and thicker in consistency. For a smooth demi-glace, strain it one last time, through a fine mesh sieve into a flat cas-serole type dish and allow to cool. Then refrigerate until the demi-glace has set. Portion the demi-glace into 3 to 4 inch squares and freeze for up to 3 months.

FOR THE BONES AND VEGETABLES

6 tablespoons soybean oil, preferably from Michigan

12 pounds veal bones

3 whole large carrots, coarsely chopped

2 whole large onions, coarsely chopped

1 head hard necked garlic, split across the equator

3 whole celery ribs, coarsely chopped

2 whole leeks, coarsely chopped

½ cup tomato paste

FOR THE STOCK

1 cup dry red wine, preferably from Michigan

1 tablespoon whole peppercorns

3 sprigs fresh thyme

4 whole bay leaves

8–10 quarts cold water

Index

aji amarillo chile peppers, 99, 178
aji amarillo powder, 108, 127, 149, 185, 188
almonds, slivered, 128
ancho chili powder, 46, 69, 82, 127, 137, 157
anchovy fillets, 18, 47
apple brandy, 78
apple cider, 46, 64, 92, 137, 181
Apple Cider Syrup/Boiled Cider, 64
apple cider vinegar, 46, 47, 55, 119
Apple Pâte Brisée, 78, 181
apple powder, 46
apples, 78, 134
apricots, dried, 67
artichoke hearts, 18, 85
artisan beer, 96, 137
artisan bread, 18, 82, 105, 125
artisan lager, 175
arugula, 63
asparagus, 39, 49
avocado, 137

bacon. See Maple Cured Hickory Smoked Bacon
Baked Michigan Navy Beans with Smoked Bacon, Chiles and Cocoa, 146
Balaton Cherries Jubilee, 52
Balaton Cherry and Michigan Maple Crisp, 50
Balaton Cherry Mojo, 53
bananas, 64
Barbecue Beef Brisket, 126
Barbecue "Mop" with Apple Cider Vinegar, Maple and Jalapeños, 45, 46
Barbecued Pork Ribs with Blueberry Chipotle Chile Rub and Blueberry Mop, 55
Barbecued Pork Shoulder with Maple Apple Rub and Cider Mop, 45
Basic Barbecue Rub, 126, 127
Basic Maple Brine, 36, 56, 108, 119, 166, 173
basil, 15, 60, 177, 185
Basil Walnut Pesto, 18, 185
bay leaves, 15, 22, 82, 126, 173
beans
    broad, 25
    great Northern white, 21, 85, 133
    green, 25
    haricots verts, 116
    navy, 146
Béchamel, Roasted Garlic, 82
beef
    brisket, 126
    broth, 126
    jerky, 161
    sirloin, 166
    steaks, 137, 143

Beef and Pork Pasty with a Classic Suet Crust, 166
beer, 96, 137, 146, 175
beet sugar, 50, 63, 77, 170, 177, 186
Beet Sugar Simple Syrup, 186
berries
    blueberries, 31, 56, 70, 74, 77
    cranberries, 70, 73, 112
    raspberries, 31, 60, 184
    strawberries, 31, 58
Beurre Manié, 82
Big Soft Pretzels, 117
biscuits, 138
bittersweet chocolate, 169
black truffles, 158
black walnuts, 58
blueberries
    dried, 70
    fresh, 31, 56, 74, 77
Blueberry and Chipotle Chile Rub, 55, 56
blueberry concentrate, 55, 77
blueberry powder, 56
bockwurst, 134
Bolivian Macaroni and Cheese, 82-83
bologna, ring, 134
brandy
    apple, 78
    cherry, 31, 52
bratwurst, 134
bread
    beer, 96
    See also artisan bread
breadcrumbs, fresh, 35, 82, 170
brine, 173
broad beans, 25
broth
    beef, 126
    chicken, 188
    poultry, 146
    vegetable, 104, 158, 183
butter
    Beurre Manié, 82
    sweet, 82, 181
    unsalted, 178
    walnut, 165
    See also Compound Butter
buttermilk, 108, 110, 132, 144, 147, 161
Buttermilk Cornmeal Waffles, 108, 110
button mushrooms, 154, 172

Camembert cheese, 70
capers, 18, 32
carnaroli rice, 158
Carrot Blueberry Juice, 74
Carrot Couscous with White Shrimp and Chives, 107
carrot juice, 107, 113
Carrot Peach Juice, 74

Carrot Watermelon Juice, 74
carrots, 35, 74, 105, 116, 126, 168, 173
caviar, 38
celery, 22, 26, 67, 105, 126, 168, 172
champagne vinegar, 179
chanterelle mushrooms, 154
cheddar cheese
    raw milk, 28
    white, 21, 84, 102, 115
Cheese Fondue with Hard Apple Cider, 125
cheese
    Camembert, 70
    Emmenthaler, 125
    goat, 49, 66
    Gruyère, 125
    Maytag Blue, 63, 149, 165, 176
    provolone, 82
    See also cheddar; mozzarella; Parmesan
cherries
    Balaton, 50, 52, 53
    dried tart, 47, 66, 67, 70, 144
cherry brandy, 31, 52
chicken
    broth, 188
    fried, 108
    poached breast, 113
    seasoned breast, 68
    skewered tenderloins, 91
    wings, 119
Chicken Fried Venison Steaks with Beef Jerky Cream Gravy, 161
Chicken Sugar Beet Skewers with Maple Smoked Jalapeño and Lime Glaze, 91
Chilled Raspberry Cream Soup, 60
Chilled Spelt, Sweet Corn and Tomato Salad, 128
chipotle chile powder, 56, 146
chives, 38, 49, 92, 105, 107, 128
chocolate
    bittersweet, 169
    cocoa, 143, 146, 169
    white, 111
Chowder Crackers, 15, 19, 175
chowders, 15, 98
cider
    apple, 46, 64, 92, 137, 181
    hard apple, 64, 70, 112, 125, 132, 134
cilantro, 19, 87, 92, 102, 137
cinnamon, Saigon, 50, 104, 143, 170
clover honey, 60, 73, 102, 180
cloves, 134, 146
cocoa powder, 143, 146, 169
coffee, espresso, 185
coffee beans, 143
Coffee Maple Glaze, 185
Compound Butter, 15, 35, 56, 95, 158, 178
corn, 39, 95, 98, 128

corn flour, 38
corn smut 84
Cornish game hen, 36
cornmeal, 38, 110, 144, 147, 168, 175, 188
Cornmeal Porridge, 188
couscous, 107
cranberries, dried, 70, 73, 112
cranberry juice, 180
Cranberry Syrup, 180
Cream of Grilled Tomato Soup, 121
Cream of Hickory Smoked Tomato Soup, 162
crème fraîche, 15, 49, 154
crimini mushrooms, 154
Crispy Hot Maple Chocolate Truffles, 170
cumin, 127, 137, 146, 157
custard, 27

Demi-Glace, 189
Dijon mustard, 36, 55, 85, 119, 182, 183
dill, 32
Double Apple Galette, 78
Double Blueberry Lime Ice Cream, 77
dry mustard powder, 56, 127, 157

eggs
    in batter, 110
    in dough, 38, 181
    hard-boiled, 32
    in ice cream, 77
    in mayonnaise, 183
    in quiche custard, 27
    scrambled, 39
    in stuffing, 105
Emmenthaler cheese, 125
espresso, 185

fajitas, 137
fennel, 105, 173
field greens, organic, 36
filé powder, 22
fish and shellfish
    mussels, 35
    perch, 41
    salmon, 32, 35
    sea scallops, 131
    shrimp, 22, 25, 92, 99, 101, 105, 107
    whitefish, 15, 16, 18, 19, 21, 22, 172
Fish Stock, 15, 172
flour
    bread, 58
    cake, 58
flour
    for quiche crust, 27
    gluten-free, 138, 141
    high gluten bread, 156
    popcorn, 101

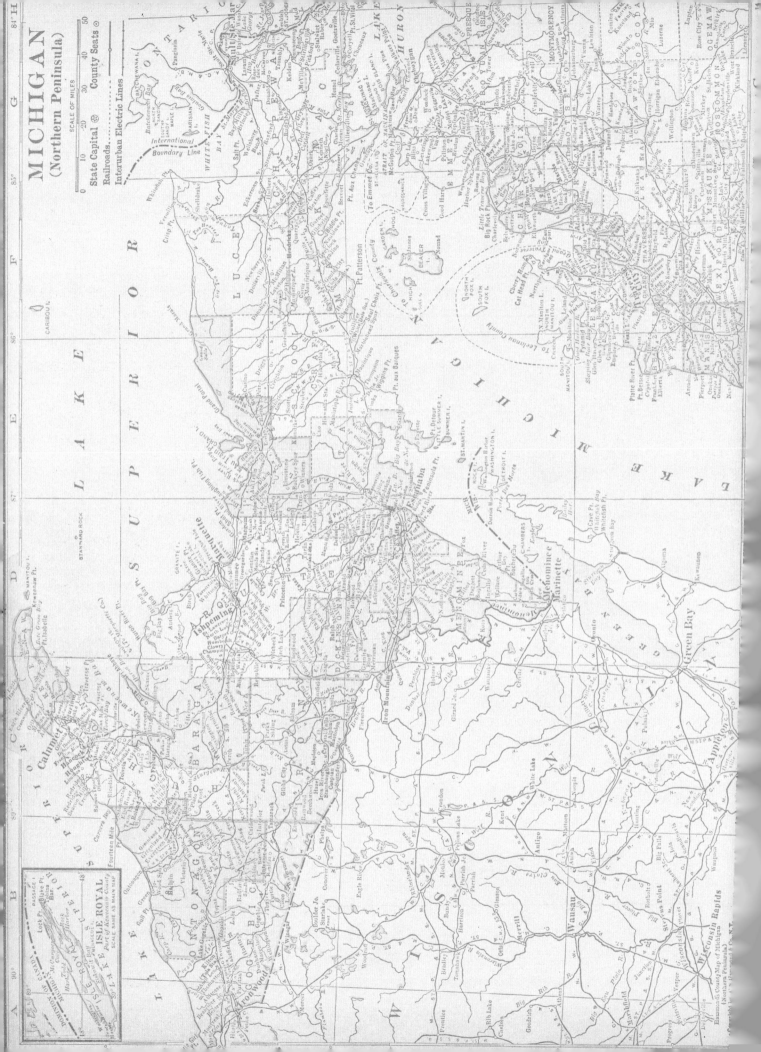

SCALE OF MILES

State Capital ⊛
County Seats ⊙
Railroads
Interurban Electric Lines

International Boundary Line